Bookcase

GW01190763

Fiction

Steve .B

Contents • Fiction

The Phantom Tollbooth

NORTON JUSTER

Chapter Four: Confusion in the Market Place

Milo receives a surprise present of a magic tollbooth. He passes through the tollbooth, into the Kingdom of Wisdom and sets out on the road to Dictionopolis. On the way he makes friends with a watchdog called Tock. Milo and Tock arrive in the city of Dictionopolis on market day, but the market is not like any market Milo's seen before.

'Get your fresh-picked ifs, ands, and buts.'

'Hey-yaa, hey-yaa, hey-yaa, nice ripe wheres and whens.'

'Juicy, tempting words for sale.'

So many words and so many people! They were from every place imaginable and some places even beyond that, and they were all busy sorting, choosing, and stuffing things into cases. As soon as one was filled, another was begun. There seemed to be no end to the bustle and activity.

Milo and Tock wandered up and down between the stalls looking at the wonderful assortment of words for sale. There were short ones and easy ones for everyday use, and long and important ones for special occasions, and even some marvellously fancy ones packed in individual gift boxes for use in royal decrees and pronouncements.

'Step right up, step right up – fancy, best-quality words right here,' announced one man in a booming voice. 'Step right up – ah, what can I do for you, little boy? How about a nice bagful of pronouns – or maybe you'd like our special assortment of names?'

Milo had never thought much about words before, but these looked so good that he longed to have some.

'Look, Tock,' he cried, 'aren't they wonderful?'

'They're fine, if you have something to say,' replied Tock in a tired voice, for he was much more interested in finding a bone than in shopping for new words.

'Maybe if I buy some I can learn how to use them,' said Milo eagerly as he began to pick through the words in the stall. Finally he chose three which looked particularly good to him – 'quagmire', 'flabbergast', and 'upholstery'. He had no idea what they meant, but they looked very grand and elegant.

'How much are these?' he enquired, and when the man whispered the answer he quickly put them back on the shelf and started to walk on.

'Why not take a few pounds of "happys?"' advised the salesman. 'They're much more practical – and very useful for Happy Birthday, Happy New Year, happy days, and happy-go-lucky.'

'I'd like to very much,' began Milo, 'but – '

'Or perhaps you'd be interested in a package of "goods" – always handy for good morning, good afternoon, good evening, and goodbye,' he suggested.

Milo did want to buy something, but the only money he had was the coin he needed to get back through the tollbooth, and Tock, of course, had nothing but the time.

'No, thank you,' replied Milo. 'We're just looking.' And they continued on through the market.

As they turned down the last lane of stalls, Milo noticed a wagon that seemed different from the rest. On its side was a small neatly lettered sign that said DO IT YOURSELF, and inside were twenty-six bins filled with all the letters of the alphabet from A to Z.

'These are for people who like to make their own words,' the man in charge informed him. 'You can pick any assortment you like or buy a special box complete with all letters, punctuation marks, and a book of instructions. Here, taste an A; they're very good.'

Milo nibbled carefully at the letter and discovered that it was quite sweet and delicious – just the way you'd expect an A to taste.

'I knew you'd like it,' laughed the letter man, popping two Gs and an R into his mouth and letting the juice drip down his chin. 'As are one of our most popular letters. All of them aren't so good,' he confided in a low voice. 'Take the Z, for instance - very dry and sawdusty. And the X? Why, it tastes like a trunkful of stale air. That's why people hardly ever use them. But most of the others are quite tasty. Try some more.'

He gave Milo an I, which was icy and refreshing, and Tock took a crisp, crunchy C.

'Most people are too lazy to make their own words,' he continued, 'but it's much more fun.'

'Is it difficult? I'm not much good at making words,' admitted Milo, spitting the pips from a P.

'Perhaps I can be of some assistance - a-s-s-i-s-t-a-n-c-e,' buzzed an unfamiliar voice, and when Milo looked up he saw an enormous bee, at least twice his size, sitting on top of the wagon.

'I am the Spelling Bee,' announced the Spelling Bee. 'Don't be alarmed - a-l-a-r-m-e-d.'

Tock ducked under the wagon, and Milo, who was not over fond of normal-sized bees, began to back away slowly.

'I can spell anything - a-n-y-t-h-i-n-g,' he boasted, testing his wings. 'Try me, try me!'

'Can you spell goodbye?' suggested Milo as he continued to back away.

The bee gently lifted himself into the air and circled lazily over Milo's head.

'Perhaps - p-e-r-h-a-p-s - you are under the misapprehension - m-i-s-a-p-p-r-e-h-e-n-s-i-o-n - that I am dangerous,' he said, turning a smart loop to the left. 'Let me assure - a-s-s-u-r-e - you that my intentions are peaceful - p-e-a-c-e-f-u-l.' And with that he settled back on top of the wagon and fanned himself with one wing. 'Now,' he panted, 'think of the most difficult word you can and I'll spell it. Hurry up, hurry up!' And he jumped up and down impatiently.

He looks friendly enough, thought Milo, not sure just how friendly a friendly bumblebee should be, and tried to think of a very difficult word.

'Spell "vegetable",' he suggested, for it was one that always troubled him at school.

'That is a difficult one,' said the bee, winking at the letter man. 'Let me see now ... hmmmmmm ... ' He frowned and wiped his brow and paced slowly back and forth on top of the wagon. 'How much time do I have?'

'Just ten seconds,' cried Milo excitedly. 'Count them off, Tock.'

'Oh dear, oh dear, oh dear, oh dear,' the bee repeated, continuing to pace nervously. Then, just as the time ran out, he spelled as fast as he could - 'v-e-g-e-t-a-b-l-e'.

'Correct,' shouted the letter man, and everyone cheered.

'Can you spell everything?' asked Milo admiringly.

'Just about,' replied the bee with a hint of pride in his voice. 'You see, years ago I was just an ordinary bee minding my own business, smelling flowers all day, and occasionally picking up part-time work in people's bonnets. Then one day I realized that I'd never amount to anything without an education and, being naturally adept at spelling, I decided that - '

'BALDERDASH!' shouted a booming voice. And from behind the wagon stepped a large beetle-ink insect dressed in a lavish coat, striped trousers, checked waistcoat, spats, and a derby hat. 'Let me repeat - BALDERDASH!' he shouted again, swinging his cane and clicking his heels in mid-air. 'Come now, don't be ill-mannered. Isn't someone going to introduce me to the little boy?'

'This,' said the bee with complete disdain, 'is the Humbug. A very dislikable fellow.'

'NONSENSE! Everyone loves a Humbug,' shouted the Humbug. 'As I was saying to the king just the other day - '

'You've never met the king,' accused the bee angrily. Then, turning to Milo, he said, 'Don't believe a thing this old fraud says.'

'BOSH!' replied the Humbug. 'We're an old and noble family, honourable to the core - *Insecticus humbugium*, if I may use the Latin. Why, we fought in the Crusades with Richard the Lionheart, crossed the Atlantic with Columbus, blazed trails with the pioneers, and today many members of the family hold prominent government positions throughout the world. History is full of Humbugs.'

'A very pretty speech - s-p-e-e-c-h,' sneered the bee. 'Now why don't you go away? I was just advising the lad of the importance of proper spelling.'

'BAH!' said the bug, putting an arm round Milo. 'As soon as you learn to spell one word, they ask you to spell another. You can never catch up – so why bother? Take my advice, my boy, and forget about it. As my great-great-great-grandfather George Washington Humbug used to say – '

'You, sir,' shouted the bee very excitedly, 'are an imposter – i-m-p-o-s-t-e-r – who can't even spell his own name.'

'A slavish concern for the composition of words is the sign of a bankrupt intellect,' roared the Humbug, waving his cane furiously.

Milo didn't have any idea what this meant, but it seemed to infuriate the Spelling Bee, who flew down and knocked off the Humbug's hat with his wing.

'Be careful,' shouted Milo as the bug swung his cane again, catching the bee on the foot and knocking over the box of Ws.

'My foot!' shouted the bee.

'My hat!' shouted the bug – and the fight was on.

The Spelling Bee buzzed dangerously in and out of range of the Humbug's wildly swinging cane as they menaced and threatened each other, and the crowd stepped back out of danger.

'There must be some other way to – ' began Milo. And then he yelled, 'WATCH OUT,' but it was too late.

There was a tremendous crash as the Humbug in his great fury tripped into one of the stalls, knocking it into another, then another, until every stall in the market place had been upset and the words lay scrambled in great confusion all over the square.

The bee, who had tangled himself in some bunting, toppled to the ground, knocking Milo over on top of him, and lay there shouting, 'Help! Help! There's a little boy on me.' The bug sprawled untidily on a mound of squashed letters and Tock, his alarm ringing persistently, was buried under a pile of words.

The Flight of the Doves

WALTER MACKEN

Chapter Ten

Finn Dove and his sister Derval are orphans, living in London with their cruel Uncle Toby. To escape their uncle, they decide to run away and search for their Granny O'Flaherty in Galway. With Derval disguised as a boy and helped by some unlikely people, they make their way across Ireland.

Finn didn't know what the name of this village was.

He left Derval near a pigsty down the lane off the street of the village. It was a clean pigsty, with small curious pigs in it. The wall was low and Derval could stand on a stone and look in at them. They looked back at her, and came close to the wall with their snouts pointed up at her, giving little grunts. There were about ten of them in it.

'You stay here,' he said. 'I'll just go to a shop and buy a few things. You are not to move.'

'I won't move,' she said, plucking a bit of grass and offering it to one of the pigs. It sniffed it and disdained it. It was well fed.

He left her.

He walked cautiously up the narrow lane. It was quite muddy but his shoes were so muddy now that it made no difference to them. They had no food at all left. For the last day and a half he had been afraid to go anywhere near a village or a small town. They had just walked the fields close to roads, hiding when they heard anybody on the road and proceeding again when they had passed. They gave all the lonely houses a wide berth, so wide indeed that they hadn't even once aroused the bark of a dog. But they hadn't travelled far this way. All the roundabout was losing miles on them. He had decided that after today they would get on a big road and walk it, in the hope that they were outside the searchers' net that would have been thrown around the countryside near the bridge. But to do that they would have to eat first.

He walked cautiously up the lane, and came on to the road and looked. It was a small village. There were only about twelve houses.

One of them, halfway up the street, was a modern shop with a big window that looked strange set into an old-fashioned house.

As he walked towards it he was fingering the money in his pocket and wondering what was the best thing to buy. Bread and butter, and some fruit, which was very dear. Maybe he should buy some eggs for Derval but they would be hard to carry without breaking, and some meat anyhow, out of a tin or cooked, so that she would have something substantial to eat. Chocolate for sure.

He looked at the window of the shop. There were so many nice things in the window that they were beginning to confuse him. But the prices were marked and he started to add up in his head how much he could afford out of his few shillings.

Determined, he walked towards the entrance. He hadn't noticed a car coming down the street, but he noticed it now, for staring at him with his mouth open was Uncle Toby.

As Uncle Toby shouted 'Stop,' to the driver who was a policeman, Finn turned and ran.

He heard the car stopping and starting again and he heard the voice of Uncle Toby calling.

He thought he would never reach the mouth of the lane. His heart was pounding madly. His breath was short, but then he was there and he turned running. Behind he heard the screech of brakes as the car stopped. It could never come down this narrow lane. He heard the voice of Uncle Toby calling, 'Finn! Finn!'

He ran around the bend. Derval was still looking in at the pigs. He grabbed her hand. 'Run! Run!' he said and pulled her after him. She couldn't run fast. How could she? She had such small legs. He knew Uncle Toby couldn't run fast either, but the policeman who was with him in the car looked young. Finn prayed that he was fat, but he didn't think so.

He had to slow down for Derval. She was running as fast as she could. The lane twisted a lot, and then they came to the place where it was bisected by a slow-moving river. The river looked clean and ran over gravel. He bent down. 'On my back!' he said to her. She put her arms around his neck, and he ran straight into the river. This was brave of him because he didn't know how deep it was. It slowed him down and he felt it wet in his shoes and his socks and up to his legs, up, up until it was past his knees.

It didn't go any higher, and he was soon free and into the lane again, and as he saw a turn off to the left he took it and ran, Derval still on his back, but there was despair in his heart, because he knew he couldn't outrun them, they were only a few minutes behind, and he was panting hard, his head down.

So he didn't see the man he ran into, but he heard the 'Oops!' a sort of grunt as they nearly knocked him down.

Finn stopped. What was the use? It was all over. He looked at the man. He wore a hat and a thick jersey and a coat and trousers tucked into his socks and he carried a pack on his back and a home-made walking-stick in his hand.

'Someone after you?' he asked.

Finn couldn't answer. He just nodded his head.

They were beside a dike that sheltered a field. There was a gate into the field, but the man didn't hesitate.

He took Derval from Finn. 'Over the dike,' he said, and went over himself, carrying Derval.

Inside the gate there was a big stack of turf that the farmer had built, for his winter supply, nicely dried by the sun, sods built up into the shape of a pan loaf. But it was deceptive, as Finn saw. The man ran to the end of it, and here there was an opening where a horse-cart rested on its shafts. Finn followed the man in here and he had to sit on the ground to recover his breath. The man let Derval down on her feet and they listened. They heard the sound of running feet and the calling voice of Uncle Toby: 'Finn! Here I am. Come to me, dear boy! Finn! Finn! It's your own Uncle Toby.'

Finn was looking at the face of the man. The hat was back off his forehead. He had a square sort of face. He was grinning. He winked at Finn. Finn didn't know why, but this wink suddenly and immediately restored all his courage.

We are not caught yet, he thought. There is still hope for us. They listened in silence as the calling voice faded away.

Finn looked at the man.

'My name is Michael,' the man said. 'I am hiking about the place. On a holiday.'

'I am Finn,' Finn said, 'and this is my sis – my brother Terry.'

'Pleased to meet you,' Michael said. 'Hello, Terry.'

Derval looked at him solemnly for a while and then she smiled.

'You don't want to meet the man who is calling your name?' Michael asked.

'No,' said Finn.

'We better move, so,' Michael said. 'Out there is a very big bog. If we can cross this bog and get to the network of roads on the other side we will have a good two days' start on them. They will stay searching this side because they won't think you could cross the bog. Will we go?'

'All right,' said Finn.

'We will keep behind the voice for a little while,' said Michael. 'Let us hope that he keeps calling.'

They came out of the carthouse cautiously, and went to the gate and listened. They could still hear the voice of Uncle Toby calling.

'Good,' Michael said and they went into the lane. They walked up the lane, still listening. Michael seemed to be able to trace the movements of the others by the sound of the voice. He stopped at the place where the river bisected the lane. This made him look at Finn's feet.

'You are very wet,' he said.

'But we are still free,' said Finn.

Michael listened once more. The sound of the voice had stopped now. 'They will go to the car now,' he said, 'and circle around the area. So we will head for the bog.'

He turned left and they followed him.

About half a mile of twisting and winding lanes were behind them when they came on to the great bog. It seemed to stretch to the horizon. Away off to the left of them they saw a big station with water-cooling towers sending great clouds of steam into the sky. Here for miles the bog was brown where it had been cut over with giant machines.

'They make electricity down there,' Michael said. 'We'll go this other way.' This was a great part of bog that was covered in heather and tufts of green sedge and on the hard ground there were furze bushes growing with yellow-coloured blossoms on them. 'Could you carry my pack?' Michael asked.

'I could,' said Finn.

'The going will be soft,' said Michael. 'I will have to carry the little brother.'

He stripped himself of the pack and put it on Finn's back. It was quite heavy. Michael tightened the straps on his shoulders, and then bent and said to Derval, 'Up now.' Derval hesitated a little but then put her arms around his neck, and he tucked her legs around his waist with his arms. 'Follow me closely,' he said to Finn.

They set off into the bog.

Finn noticed that he chose low ground between little hillocks, so that if anybody was looking out over the bog from a height they would be hidden by the folds. This low ground was very wet and soggy. Now and again they came on sort of roads that had been built into the bog from the sides. Here there were turf banks, with bogholes in front of them, where men still cut out turf with the slean, and you could see the marks of the slean in the high banks.

Finn didn't know how many miles they had travelled, but the pack on his back seemed to get heavier and heavier. The sun was behind a mist and it was very hot. There was no wind. The bog-larks were high in the sky, singing. It was almost impossible to see them. Now and again fluttering snipe got up almost from under their feet.

His eyes were almost closed with the tiredness when he heard Michael say, 'We will stop here.'

He looked around him. It was a place where turf-cutters had been working. There were freshly cut sods of turf laid out in long rows to dry. The turf-cutters had made themselves comfortable when they were there. They had cut a sort of cave out of last year's high bank. There were three railway sleepers around the three sides of it, and it was floored with dry heather and last year's sedge. In front of it there was a hearth they had made with stones, and the white ashes of former turf fires were still there.

'You are tired, Terry,' Michael said to her.

'Oh, no,' she said.

'Here,' he said. 'You go into this nice cave and lie on the bench.' He brought her in. He had felt her head nodding on his back as he carried her. 'You lie down there for a little while,' he said. 'And we'll cook up something good for you.' He stripped off his own coat and put it on the bench. She climbed up without his assistance and lay down. Almost while he was looking at her she was asleep.

'Change your pants,' he said to Finn. 'Have you a change with you?'

'I have another trousers and socks,' said Finn.

'Change,' said Michael. 'I'll light a fire and you can dry them.'

Finn went into the cave and opened his bundle.

Michael got last year's turf from around the bank and in no time at all he had a turf fire going. Finn watched in amazement as he took a kettle and a pan from the pack. He went and collected water from a little trickle that was flowing from the ground into a boghole.

When the fire was going well, he broadened it so that it would hold both the kettle and the pan, and then he proceeded to take huge chunks of steak from the pack and he put those on the pan. Also he had three plastic plates and three plastic cups. Idly it entered into Finn's head why he should have three of those things, but the smell of the cooking was so pleasant that the saliva started to run from his teeth. Michael had bread and butter, and when the steaks were nearly done, he plopped thick slices of bread into the hot fat.

He was laughing at the look on Finn's face.

'Why are you laughing?' Finn asked.

'You look so hungry,' he said.

'Why do you have such good things when you are hiking?' Finn asked.

'It's only young hikers,' said Michael, 'that don't think of their stomachs. When I hike, I like to hike in comfort. Will your brother come out now? At this stage, I think he needs food more than sleep.'

Later they sat in front of the fire. Their seats were sods of dried turf packed together. They made nice enough seats. Finn thought he had never tasted better food in his life. It was coming on to twilight time. The fire was making their faces glow.

Michael was smoking a cigarette. Then he put his hand in his back pocket and took out a paper.

'Read that, Finn,' he said.

Finn looked at him, startled, and then he looked at the newspaper.

GRANNY O'FLAHERTY DEFIANT, it said.

It went on to say that the flying Doves were still at liberty despite an intense police search and the offering of a reward. Mrs Grainne O'Flaherty, the grandmother of the children, had been asked if she would shelter the children if they succeeded in reaching her. She said she didn't give a traneen for their supposed guardian or the supposed guardianship of the courts. If her grandchildren reached her, nobody would take them away except over her dead body. Asked if they were with her now, she replied that even an O'Flaherty Dove couldn't fly that fast. She was expecting them every day at Carraigmore.

'That's it,' said Finn involuntarily, 'that's the name, Carraigmore.' Then he put his hand over his mouth as he looked at Michael. Then he took it down. 'Do you know?' he asked.

'It would be hard for me not to,' Michael said. 'You bump into me. I read the papers. You have red hair.'

'But why are you helping us, so,?' asked Finn.

'How do I know?' Michael asked. 'I don't like people chasing kids or something. What does it matter? We'll sleep here tonight. We'll finish crossing the bog tomorrow, and then we will part and you'll go your way and I'll go mine. Isn't that fair enough?'

'You will go away?' Derval asked suddenly.

'I have to,' he said. 'You will be going west, and I will be going east. I have people to see. But who knows, maybe our paths will cross again.'

'I'm sorry you are not coming with us to Granny,' said Derval.

'You have nothing to worry about,' said Micheal. 'Finn will look after you. He is doing very well.'

'If it wasn't for you we would have been caught,' said Finn.

'How do you know?' Michael asked. 'Something else might have happened. You might have got away. If a fellow wants a thing badly enough, he will get it. Will you tell me why you want so badly to get to Carraigmore?'

Finn looked at him. Michael's eyes were calm and kind, he thought. He wouldn't be a one to go and tell the police he saw you for the sake of a hundred pounds. He picked up a piece of turf and rolled it between his hands.

Then he tried to explain to Michael why he wanted to get to Carraigmore.

Well, he has convinced me, anyhow, Michael thought, and it was as well that I caught up with him. Looking at the thin earnest face, with the freckled nose and the firm chin, and hearing the unexaggerated account of life with Uncle Toby, he was glad he had made his decision. But this was not the end of the road. There was a long way between here and Carraigmore and the law and courts were powerful things, very difficult to circumvent.

He could put them in a car now and deliver them to Granny O'Flaherty. But that would be breaking the law, and after all he was the law. He was bending the law now but not breaking it or he would have to resign from the police. He intended to cross the sea, meet the Inspector, and investigate Uncle Toby, talk to his neighbours,

and find out what was compelling him in the pursuit of the children. He couldn't believe it was love, somehow. Because the arm of the law was long, and it would reach out for the children no matter where they ended up. Even if he brought them straight to their destination now, the law would be there.

He would have to be prepared to meet the law with the truth. This was what the law was about. Truth had no law to fight. He hoped the children could keep free for the time required to find the truth that would really free them. He thought, with Finn's determination, that they might.

'I will have to leave you in the morning,' he said. He saw that Finn was upset. 'I must,' he said. 'It will only be for a few days. I want to find out important things that will be good for you in the long run. But I will catch up with you again.'

'You will?' said Finn.

'I promise,' he said. 'You'll see me again when you least expect me.'

Then he gave Finn a better map, marked.

'Don't follow the railroad,' he said. 'They will be watching that. Go north from the railroad, and get across the Shannon away from the railroad. You see the river. There are different bridges. They will be watching the bridges.' He waited until he was sure Finn knew the best route. 'When you cross the river and get into the mountains, Granny O'Flaherty will be reaching out for you.'

Next morning when they crossed the bog and got on to the roads on the other side, he left them. They were sorry to see him go, but out of his pack he had loaded their own bags with food and tins, enough to keep them going for a few days.

They waved goodbye after him.

I don't care, Finn was thinking, I am going to get to Carraigmore.

They set out to walk west. Michael sat down to wait until they were out of sight.

The Animal, the Vegetable and John D. Jones

BETSY BYARS

Chapter Twenty-Two

Clara and Deanie are on holiday with their divorced father; the holiday is not going very well. When they are joined by his girlfriend Delores and her son, John D., things go from bad to worse.

John D. and his mother sat on the plastic sofa in the office of the Coast Guard. The cushions were stiff and uneven, and they sat on the edge of their seats like unwanted guests. A cup of cold coffee was in his mother's hand, forgotten.

At the desk, waiting by the radio, were Deanie and her father. He was leaning forward, hand over his eyes as if shielding them from too much light. His shoulders were hunched up stiffly under his thin shirt. Deanie was twisting her hair.

'What did the man say?' Deanie asked as a garbled message came from the radio. Both she and her father leaned forward.

'It wasn't about your daughter, sir,' the man answered in a kind voice.

'Why can't they find her?'

'Every ship we have is on alert, every fishing boat's been contacted, two helicopters are searching the area.'

'I know, but she can't have got that far. It's only been three hours.'

'They know where to look, sir. They know the tides.' He paused. 'I'll let you know as soon as we hear something.' He waited as if he expected them to move away, but they remained hunched miserably over the desk.

Across the room, Delores sighed. 'I absolutely cannot bear to think of Clara out there on a flimsy raft. She must be terrified.'

'I should think,' John D. answered tersely.

'You know,' her voice lowered, 'I have always had a real dread of the ocean. I admit it. I have the feeling when I'm swimming that there are, I don't know, *creatures* under there.'

'There are, Mother.'

'And the thought of being out there out there on a raft!' Her voice lowered again. 'John D., that kind of raft costs five dollars. It is made of the cheapest, flimsiest plastic there is!'

'I know!' John D. always spoke with special anger when his mother said exactly what he himself was thinking.

'I should never have let her go out.'

'Mom, it was not your fault.' He got up abruptly and walked to the desk. He stood behind Deanie, waiting to be noticed.
'Any news?' he asked finally.

Deanie glanced around. In her anxiety she had twisted her hair into long uneven curls, and her face looked like something out of an old album. 'No,' she said. John D. waited a moment more, then turned and walked to the window. He looked out.

Beyond the bay and the tidal marsh and the live oaks and the palmettos, the sun was beginning to sink in the sky.

John D. watched as it moved closer to the tree tops, and turned the water red.

The boats rose and fell in the marina. White yachts, sailboats, double-decker cruisers, old fishing boats, all wallowed on the waves. The water was getting rougher, John D. noticed.

He crossed the room, got a drink of water he didn't want and sat by his mother. He flopped down so hard that his mother bounced.

'No news?' she asked.

'No.'

His mother took a sip of her cold coffee. 'It has always bothered me terribly to think of somebody who is trapped. I can hardly read stories about people who are stuck in mines or submarines. And now Clara - I can't bear it.'

She broke off as another message came over the radio. The operator looked up and shook his head. It was not about Clara.

'There was a dreadful story last summer,' she went on. 'A man, in the Pacific, I believe, fell overboard, and ship after ship went right past him. A liner almost bumped into him.'

'That won't happen with Clara,' he said. He sometimes felt that in hard times he and his mother switched places. He became the calming adult saying, 'That won't happen,' and 'Everything will be all right,' while she thought up new worries.

'I should never have let her go out on that raft.'

'Mom.'

'I shouldn't have. I did a whole column on it once – on not letting your child's life depend on a two dollar piece of inflated plastic. I had had this heart-breaking letter from a woman whose child – they were in a lake – and she turned her back just for a moment and – '

'Mom.'

'You know why I didn't?' She paused. 'Because I wanted the girls to like me, and I was afraid if I kept saying over and over, "Be careful. Don't do this. Stop that," well, only look! They don't like me at all.'

'They like you.'

'They don't. So I might as well have played the part of the Wicked Stepmother. At least Clara would be safer.'

The radio was transmitting again, and the operator leaned close. Deanie and her father strained to hear. John D. got up quickly and crossed the room.

'Go ahead … yes … '

Clara's father drew his shoulders up under his thin shirt as if he were prepared to take a blow. Deanie reached for his arm.

'I see … How far out? … What colour was it? … Any sign of the girl? … I see.'

There was a long pause, then the man said, 'Discontinue search.'

'What?' Deanie asked in the sudden stillness. 'Discontinue?'

The man remained at the silent radio, bent forward, eyes on the dials. Then he looked up at Clara's father. He took off his cap. He made a gesture with his head, a sideways nod, as if he were trying to rid himself of a troubling thought.

'The helicopter spotted the raft,' he said. 'Your daughter wasn't on it.'

Tom's Midnight Garden

PHILIPPA PEARCE

Chapter Three

Tom is staying with his uncle and aunt who live in a strange old house. One night, Tom decides to explore.

Tom opened the door wide and let in the moonlight. It flooded in, as bright as daylight – the white daylight that comes before the full rising of the sun. The illumination was perfect, but Tom did not at once turn to see what it showed him of the clock-face. Instead he took a step forward on to the doorstep. He was staring, at first in surprise, then with indignation, at what he saw outside. That they should have deceived him – lied to him – like this! They had said, 'It's not worth your while going out at the back, Tom.' So carelessly they had described it: 'A sort of back-yard, very poky, with rubbish bins. Really, there's nothing to see.'

Nothing ... Only this: a great lawn where flower-beds bloomed; a towering fir-tree, and thick, beetle-browed yews that humped their shapes down two sides of the lawn; on the third side, to the right, a greenhouse almost the size of a real house; from each corner of the lawn, a path that twisted away to some other depths of garden, with other trees.

Tom had stepped forward instinctively, catching his breath in surprise; now he let his breath out in a deep sigh. He would steal out here tomorrow, by daylight. They had tried to keep this from him, but they could not stop him now – not his aunt, nor his uncle, nor the back flat tenants, nor even particular Mrs Bartholomew. He would run full tilt over the grass, leaping the flower-beds; he would peer through the glittering panes of the greenhouse – perhaps open the door and go in; he would visit each alcove and archway clipped in the yew-trees – he would climb the trees and make his way from one to another through thickly interlacing branches. When they came calling him, he would hide, silent and safe as a bird, among this richness of leaf and bough and tree-trunk.

The scene tempted him even now: it lay so inviting and clear before him – clear-cut from the stubby leaf-pins of the nearer yew-trees to the curled-back petals of the hyacinths in the crescent-shaped corner beds. Yet Tom remembered his ten hours

and his honour. Regretfully he turned from the garden, back indoors to read the grandfather clock.

He re-crossed the threshold, still absorbed in the thought of what he had seen outside. For that reason, perhaps, he could not at once make out how the hall had become different: his eyes informed him of some shadowy change; his bare foot was trying to tell him something …

The grandfather clock was still there, anyway, and must tell him the true time. It must be either twelve or one: there was no hour in between. There is no thirteenth hour.

Tom never reached the clock with his inquiry, and may be excused for forgetting, on this occasion, to check its truthfulness. His attention was distracted by the opening of a door down the hall – the door of the ground-floor front flat. A maid trotted out.

Tom had seen housemaids only in pictures, but he recognised the white apron, cap and cuffs, and the black stockings. (He was not an expert in fashions, but the dress seemed to him to be rather long for her.) She was carrying paper, kindling wood and a box of matches.

He had only a second in which to observe these things. Then he realised that he ought to take cover at once; and there was no cover to take. Since he must be seen, Tom determined to be the first to speak – to explain himself.

He did not feel afraid of the maid: as she came nearer, he saw that she was only a girl. To warn her of his presence without startling her, Tom gave a cough; but she did not seem to hear it. She came on. Tom moved forward into her line of vision; she looked at him, but looked through him, too, as though he were not there. Tom's heart jumped in a way he did not understand. She was passing him.

'I say!' he protested loudly; but she paid not the slightest attention. She passed him, reached the front door of the ground-floor back flat, turned the door-handle and went in. There was no bell-ringing or unlocking of the door.

Tom was left gaping; and, meanwhile, his senses began to insist upon telling him of experiences even stranger than this encounter. His one bare foot was on cold flagstone, he knew; yet there was a contradictory softness and warmth to this flagstone. He looked down and saw that he was standing on a rug – a tiger-skin rug. There were other rugs down the hall. His eyes now took in the whole of the hall – a hall that was different. No laundry box, no milk bottles, no travel posters on the walls. The walls were decorated with a rich variety of other objects instead: a tall Gothic barometer, a fan of peacock feathers, a huge engraving of a battle (hussars and horses and shot-riddled banners) and many other pictures. There was a big dinner gong, with its wash-leathered gong-stick hanging beside it. There was a large umbrella stand holding umbrellas and walking-sticks and a parasol and an air-gun and what looked like the parts of a fishing-rod. Along the wall projected a series of bracket-shelves, each table-high. They were of oak, except for one towards the middle of the hall, by the grandfather clock. That was of white marble, and it was piled high with glass cases of stuffed birds and animals. Enacted on its chilly surface were scenes of hot bloodshed: an owl clutched a mouse in its claws; a ferret looked up from the killing of its rabbit; in a case in the middle a red fox slunk along with a gamefowl hanging from its jaws.

In all that crowded hall, the only object that Tom recognised was the grandfather clock. He moved towards it, not to read its face, but simply to touch it – to reassure himself that this at least was as he knew it.

His hand was nearly upon it, when he heard a little breath behind him that was the maid passing back the way she had come. For some reason, she did not seem to make as much sound as before. He heard her call only faintly: 'I've lit the fire in the parlour.'

She was making for the door through which she had first come, and, as Tom followed her with his eyes, he received a curious impression: she reached the door, her hand was upon the knob, and then she seemed to go. That was it exactly: she went, but not through the door. She simply thinned out, and went.

Even as he stared at where she had been, Tom became aware of something going on furtively and silently about him. He looked round sharply, and caught the hall in the act of emptying itself of furniture and rugs and pictures. They were not positively going, perhaps, but rather beginning to fail to be there. The Gothic barometer, for instance, was there, before he turned to look at the red fox; when he turned back, the barometer was still there, but it had the appearance of something only sketched against the wall, and the wall was visible through it; meanwhile the fox had slunk into nothingness, and all the other creatures were going with him; and, turning back again swiftly to the barometer, Tom found that gone already.

In a matter of seconds the whole hall was as he had seen it on his first arrival. He stood dumbfounded. He was roused from his stupefaction by the chill of a draught at his back: it reminded him that the garden door was left open. Whatever else had happened, he had really opened that door; and he must shut it. He must go back to bed.

He closed the door after a long look: 'I shall come back,' he promised silently to the trees and the lawn and the greenhouse.

Upstairs, again, in bed, he pondered more calmly on what he had seen in the hall. Had it been a dream? Another possible explanation occurred to him: ghosts. That was what they could all have been: ghosts. The hall was haunted by the ghost of a housemaid and a barometer and a stuffed fox and a stuffed owl and by the ghosts of dozens of other things. Indeed, if it were haunted at all, the hall was overhaunted.

Ghosts ... Tom doubtfully put his hand up out of the bedclothes to see if his hair were standing on end. It was not. Nor, he remembered, had he felt any icy chill when the maid had looked at him and through him.

He was dissatisfied with his own explanation, and suddenly sick of needing to explain at all. It was not as if the hall were of great interest, with or without a maid and all the rest; the garden was the thing. That was real. Tomorrow he would go into it: he almost had the feel of tree-trunks between his hands as he climbed; he could almost smell the heavy blooming of the hyacinths in the corner beds. He remembered that smell from home: indoors, from his mother's bulb pots, at Christmas and the New Year; outside, in their flower-bed, in the late spring. He fell asleep thinking of home.

Timesnatch

Robert Swindells

Chapter One

Butterflies don't know much. This one didn't know it was a chequered skipper - one of only sixty left in the world. It didn't know that this sun-dappled clearing was part of Rockingham Forest, and it certainly didn't know that its quick, darting flight was closely observed by three humans, two of whom weren't even born yet.

Heavy with the eggs it bore, the insect alighted on a leaf. At once the surrounding air became suffused with a soft, pulsating glow. The leaf trembled for an instant ever so faintly and when it stopped, the butterfly had gone.

'There you go, folks.' Harper Rye held up the flask for her children to see. 'One chequered skipper, extinct for twenty years yet very much alive, undamaged and beautifully pregnant. We've finally cracked it, my darlings.'

'Oh, Mum!' Kizzy, a ten-year-old version of her mother with the same straight dark hair and glasses, flung her arms round Harper's neck and kissed her on the mouth. 'I knew you'd do it. I *always* knew.'

'Steady!' Harper set down the flask before returning the child's embrace. 'Of course you did, my precious. Your faith in your old mum has been positively unswerving.'

'I knew you'd do it too,' growled Frazer. At thirteen he was less demonstrative than his sister and more cynical. 'What I *didn't* know was that you'd get all excited over butterflies and stuff when you could be snatching people. I mean, why can't we bring *Granny* back or something?'

Harper's grin faded as she looked at her son. 'Because, my love, the ability to create new technology carries with it heavy responsibilities. If we were to misuse my invention it might cause untold harm. For example, to snatch a human being - any human being - could alter history in some dramatic way we haven't even dreamed of. No.' She shook her head. 'Rule one *must* be - no humans.'

Frazer raked a hand through his mop of ginger curls. 'Hmmm. Never thought of that, Mum. Altering history, I mean. So that's why we're sticking to animals and plants - because that won't change history?'

'It *will*,' smiled Harper, 'but hopefully not in ways which will be harmful, or even particularly noticeable.'

Kizzy gazed at her mother's machine - a machine which could vanish and reappear like something in a magic show. It reminded her of an enormous doughnut. In fact, she'd christened it 'the Doughnut' without telling the other two. 'It's absolutely fantastic, Mum,' she breathed. 'What will you call it?'

'Oh - Rye's Apparatus, I expect. It's got a sort of ring to it, don't you think?'

Kizzy nodded. Better than the Doughnut, she thought.

'Rye's Apparatus.' Frazer rolled the words across his tongue a couple of times, then nodded. 'Ye-es. That sounds suitably historic, Ma - like Parkinson's Disease and Sod's Law. I reckon it'll do.'

Harper Rye laughed. 'I don't know about historic, my love. It might be best to keep this whole thing to ourselves, at least for the time being, but I know one thing - we'd better get this poor insect to Northamptonshire or it'll be forced to deposit its precious eggs in entirely the wrong place.'

Chapter Two

It had begun four years earlier when physicist Harper Rye had noticed that certain subatomic particles were apparently capable of travelling back through time. At six, Kizzy had found the word 'physicist' too much to handle. As far as she was concerned, Mummy was a fizzy sister – a category which seemed to the child to describe her mother perfectly.

The initial discovery had given birth to an idea which had gripped Harper Rye, becoming almost an obsession. This in turn had triggered a successful application for funding to her old university, and a four-year bout of nonstop work which had driven her husband out of the family home in this isolated part of Suffolk and left the children very much to their own devices. For a couple of years they'd had a sort of nanny – a slow, amiable teenager named Pam who'd come from the village each morning to wash, dress and feed them, escort them to and from school and play with them, till she'd fallen in love and gone off to start a family of her own. They'd missed Pam terribly at first, but they'd learned to cope between them when Mum was busy, so that by the time Kizzy could say 'physicist' they were virtually independent.

Harper Rye's discovery had enabled her, after a tremendous amount of work, to design and construct a device which would travel back through time, snatch objects and convey them to her laboratory. The objects she intended to choose were plants and animals which once, not long ago, had inhabited the Earth but which had either been hunted or fished to extinction or wiped out by twentieth-century pesticides, urbanisation or pollution. Her idea was to bring male and female specimens of such creatures into the cleaner, greener present, breed from them and release the offspring into the wild. In this way the consequences of past mistakes – of man's ecological vandalism – might be redeemed. Plants and animals which had vanished forever would reappear in 2039, enriching the earth once more with their variety.

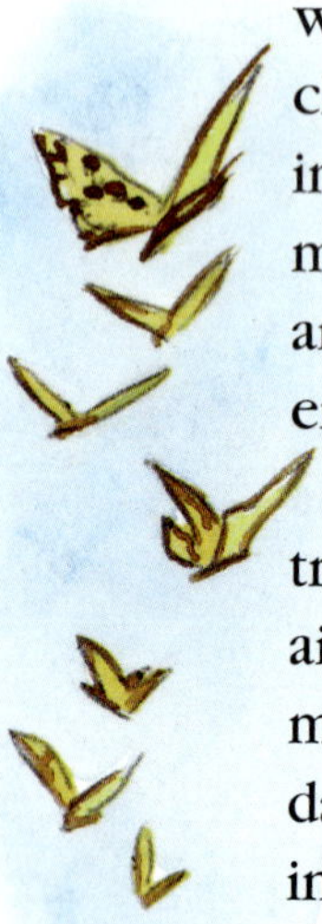

And she'd done it, but not at first. At first, she'd encountered tremendous problems. There'd been problems of accuracy – of aiming her device at exactly the right spot at precisely the correct moment to capture a specimen. Then there'd been the problem of damage – precious specimens had arrived mangled or dead, or else in such a state of shock that they'd expired within a short time.

One by one the problems had been overcome, till now Harper Rye could guarantee to capture unharmed a creature as tiny, as fast-moving and as fragile as the chequered skipper which now rested inside its flask, the only chequered skipper in the world, as she drove the family car westward along the A428 into Northamptonshire.

Chapter Three

'Why d'you say we shouldn't tell anybody about your apparatus, Mum?' They'd released the butterfly and were cruising eastwards with the setting sun in the rearview mirror. The woman reached up and adjusted the glass till she lost the glare and found Frazer's puzzled face.

'You've read some history,' she said. 'Consider the fate of inventions. The aeroplane, for example. The first plane flew in nineteen hundred and three. The two guys who designed it probably thought they were giving the world a new, exciting sport or a fast, convenient means of getting from A to B. What they *didn't* foresee was that people would load bombs and guns on their machine and use it to slaughter one another, but that's exactly what they did.'

'Oh, yeah,' protested Frazer. 'But that was dead obvious, wasn't it? I mean, they should've known that would happen. I don't see how anybody could use Rye's Apparatus in a bad way.'

His mother smiled. '*You* don't see, darling, but believe me there are those out there who might.' She laughed briefly. 'You put an invention on the market – practically any invention – and somebody will find a way to use it as a weapon or to throw people out of work or to pollute the environment. When it comes to cruelty, greed and sheer stupidity, human ingenuity knows no bounds.'

Frazer pulled a face. 'Charming.'

'What'll happen to the butterfly?' asked Kizzy. The conversation was boring her. Her mother smiled. 'Well, my love, if we're lucky – *if* we're lucky – the butterfly will lay her eggs on a leaf. Hundreds of eggs. The eggs will hatch into hundreds of caterpillars, and some of those caterpillars – nine or ten perhaps – will survive to become butterflies next year. Those butterflies will mate and lay eggs and, before you know it, there'll be hundreds of chequered skippers in

Rockingham Forest, just as there were a hundred years ago. But if we're *un*lucky,' she chuckled, 'a sparrow will eat our butterfly for breakfast first thing tomorrow morning.'

'Aw, Mu-um!'

'Well, darling, these things happen. We shan't know for ages, of course – a couple of years at least. Then, if no chequered skippers have been reported in the forest, we shall have to do the whole thing again.'

Frazer frowned. 'There's something I don't get.'

'*What* don't you get, dear?'

'The chequered skipper's extinct, right?'

'It *was*, yes.'

'Well – if it suddenly turns up again, won't people be curious? I mean, once a creature's extinct it's gone forever, isn't it?'

'Absolutely. But you see, darling, with something as tiny as the chequered skipper it's terribly hard to be certain. Nobody's *seen* one for twenty years, but when the species reappears they'll assume a few must've survived in a remote spot somewhere – that it wasn't extinct after all. That's why I chose to begin with something tiny.'

'Right.' Frazer grinned. 'It wouldn't work with a rhinoceros, would it?'

Harper shook her head. 'Not in Northamptonshire.'

They cruised on into the dusk, laughing.

No Gun for Asmir

CHRISTOBEL MATTINGLY

Chapter One

Asmir comes from Bosnia Herzegovina. That name twists the tongues of people who do not know it. But Asmir was born in Sarajevo. And it rolls off his tongue like the smooth creamy sauce and the tender tasty meat of his grandmother's *musaka*.

Asmir remembers how the mountains rose sparkling with snow in the winter all around Sarajevo. And in the summer the trees swept like green waves up the slopes. The domed roofs of the mosques gleamed like moons among the houses and the minarets spiked the skyline. Morning, noon and evening the *muezzins*' call to prayer used to echo out across the city.

Asmir's father, Muris, was a lawyer in Sarajevo. Asmir's mother, Mirsada, was a chemical engineer in a chocolate factory. Asmir's brother Eldar was still only a baby, just twelve months old.

But Asmir had many other playmates. They used to meet each day in the park near their homes, running among the trees, chasing, hiding, swinging, see-sawing, rolling on the grass, calling, laughing.

Until one day, war came to Sarajevo. Hundreds of soldiers arrived, firing rifles, firing guns. Tanks rumbled through the street. Aircraft flew over the city dropping bombs.

The smell of burning made Asmir's stomach sick. The smoke made his eyes sting. The sight of his friend the postman lying on the street with all the letters spilling out of his bag made his heart shudder. It was too late to help the postman. Asmir gathered up the bloodstained letters. But when he took them to some of the addresses, the houses were burning heaps or hollow holes. He ran home clutching the crumpled envelopes.

His grandmother washed his hands and cooked him *ustipci*. They were his favourite. But that day he could not swallow. The pancakes stuck in his throat.

Morning and night the tanks rumbled and the rockets exploded. Midday the sky filled with droning planes and the crack of snipers' rifles. There was no electricity to amplify the *muezzins*' call. It seemed to Asmir as if the soldiers had bombed God.

Then they bombed the chocolate factory. The smell of the chocolate choked Asmir to the bottom of his lungs and made his stomach churn. The chocolate burned but his mother came home. Asmir hugged her tight, and that night he crept into bed between her and his father. And the bad dreams went away.

Day after day, night after night, week after week the war went on. Grandmother came to live with them because her apartment was gone. Meat became a treat, eggs were as scarce as hens' teeth. Of course there was no chocolate. And no ice cream or lemonade either. Then there was no milk.

The daffodils were dancing in the park. The cherry trees were frothing white like the milk Asmir's father had loved on top of his coffee. But the playground had become a bomb crater and a cemetery. Two of Asmir's friends had been killed there. Another was in hospital. He would walk again if he was given an artificial leg.

'Mirsada, there are no medicines left in the hospitals and no pain-killing drugs. You must go somewhere safe with the children,' Muris said to Asmir's mother. 'It's time for you to leave while you can. They're still letting women and children go. But tonight could be the last time they do.'

Asmir saw his mother's face go pale and watched her dark eyes grow even darker. They looked like black holes of emptiness. She gripped her husband's hands. 'But Eldar has a fever. Can't we go tomorrow when he is better?'

'It's still safer in Serbia. You must go to your sister Melita in Belgrade,' Muris said. Asmir loved his aunt Melita.

His father said to him, 'Pack your holiday rucksack with your favourite toys and some for Eldar too. And help your mother choose some clothes. You can't take everything.'

Asmir put in their teddies, his best Lego and a bag of little farm animals, Eldar's cart and horse on wheels, a boat for the bath, some books, his coloured pencils and drawing pad. His mother crammed T-shirts, jeans, shorts, pyjamas, shoes and socks into a case.

Eldar was so restless that his mother slept beside him that night. So Asmir slept with his father. It was good to snuggle up with him. 'Why do we have to go away?' he asked. 'I don't want to leave you. Can't you come with us?'

'I wish I could,' his father said, 'But the war is getting worse every day. Yugoslavia is broken up. Serbia wants to take over Bosnia. That's why their army has invaded us.'

Invade. It was a crushing word. Asmir felt pinned down by it. As his friend had been by the falling wall.

His father went on, 'And women and children must have first chance to escape.'

Escape. A scary, running word. Almost worse than invade. His friend whose leg had been torn off by shrapnel couldn't run. He couldn't even walk. He couldn't escape.

'Why do we have to escape? Who are we escaping from?' Asmir's voice came out as a whisper in the dark.

'We're Muslim, Asmir. And they want to clean us out.'

'But we're clean already,' Asmir said, thinking of the washing dancing on the line, the gleaming copper cooking pots his grandmother loved to scour, the shining tiled floor, the crisp fresh clothes he put on each day. He stroked the smooth soft sheet. It was as soft as his grandmother's cheeks. And nobody could be cleaner than she was. 'Why do they want to clean us out? They're going about it in a very messy stupid way.'

He thought of the shattered glass, the piles of rubble, the splintered doors and sagging beams of houses in their own street, the proud trees in the playground blasted, split, stripped of their dancing leaves, dying.

'Who are they, anyway?'

His father groaned with a sigh that seemed to come from somewhere deeper than the graves Asmir had seen men digging in his park, even deeper than the bomb crater. 'Lots of them were our friends, Asmir. Some of them were our neighbours. Your mother and I went to school and university with some of them. Your grandmother played with their parents.'

'Then why are they fighting? It doesn't make sense.'

'War never does make sense,' Asmir's father said sadly. Asmir shivered and snuggled closer to him.

'Innocent people get hurt. Coming home from work one day your mother and I were caught between gunfire from both sides. We worry what would happen to you and Eldar if we were hurt.'

Asmir shuddered and tried to blot out the picture of the postman from his mind – so still, so crumpled. So bloody. 'Will they make you fight and kill people too?'

The words stuck in his throat. Like the pancakes had.

'They'll make some people. But I don't want to kill anyone, Asmir. I'll volunteer to work in the hospital. They'll need every pair of hands they can get to care for the wounded.'

'I wish I could stay and help you,' Asmir said.

'You have a job to do too,' his father said. 'You'll have to look after your mother and Eldar and grandmother now.'

'When will we come back?'

'I don't know. I only wish I did.'

Asmir suddenly felt old. Old and heavy. And very tired. His father put his arms around him. And that was all that mattered now. He fell asleep on his father's shoulder.

When he woke, the sunbeams were shimmering with dancing dust. Asmir coughed. There was always dust now from the bombing. He shivered. The bed was cold. He turned over. The bed was empty. 'Daddy,' he called. But there was no answer. Muris was gone.

Western Wind

PAULA FOX

Chapter One

Six months after Elizabeth Benedict was born, her grandmother, Cora Ruth Benedict, moved to Maine. Now, eleven years later, Elizabeth was to spend the month of August with her on a small island in Penobscot Bay she had never seen, in a cottage without electricity or plumbing.

'What is there to do there? What will I *do*?' Elizabeth asked her father, Charles.

'There'll be plenty to do: swim – '

'Swim! I know about Maine swimming. You turn into a tray of ice cubes as soon as you stick your toe into that water,' she said.

'The water is warmer in the coves,' Daddy said.

'Coves!' exclaimed Elizabeth scornfully.

Daddy laughed. 'That's the first time I ever heard *cove* used as a swear word.'

'What about food? Or do we live off the land?' Elizabeth asked.

Daddy ignored her sarcastic words. 'There's a boat that comes to the island once a week from Molytown on the mainland. It'll bring groceries and mail – and we'll expect weekly letters from you.'

'Groceries? Canned corn ... stale bread,' Elizabeth muttered.

'You have a poor attitude about this, my girl. You love Gran. Don't you? What's eating you?'

Elizabeth flushed and turned away. Love had nothing to do with it. She began to turn the pages of a law journal on a nearby table. Daddy knew what was eating her. She wasn't going to put into words what she felt – he would argue with her then, the way he probably did in court.

She glanced at him over her shoulder. He was staring at her. She was startled by his expression, how uncertain he looked, as though he'd stumbled on evidence that didn't fit his case.

'I was going on the bicycle trip with Nancy to New Hampshire,' she said. 'I've been thinking about it for months.'

She turned to face her father, feeling a faint hope she might still persuade him to go back to the original plan for August.

'The trip was only for a week. You can do that any summer. You're going to Gran, and that's that,' he said matter-of-factly.

'Found guilty,' Elizabeth said under her breath.

Her father smiled. She recognised the powerful grown-up smile of a parent who has made up his mind absolutely.

She started across the room to the door of the study.

'Where are you going?' he asked pleasantly.

'To pack winter clothes for August in Maine,' she said as coolly as she dared.

Old Mrs Benedict was not a grandmother in name only, as some of her friends' grandmothers were. Elizabeth, her father, her mother, Emilia, and Gran had visited each other as far back as she could remember. The younger Benedicts would go to Maine for a week or so as soon as Elizabeth's school closed for summer recess. They stayed in a bed-and-breakfast inn outside of Camden, where Gran had a small apartment overlooking a street which, she told Elizabeth, filled up with snow in winter and tourists in summer.

Ten years ago, Gran started renting the cottage on the island during July and August. It was a good place for a painter, she said. None of the Benedicts had visited her there. It was too hard to get to, Gran insisted, and it certainly wasn't big enough for four people. 'We'd go mad!' she'd said.

'Why does she need two places at her age?' Elizabeth heard her father ask her mom. 'In some ways, she's as extravagant as an adolescent.'

'She's a painter,' her mother had replied. 'They never grow older than the age at which they began to paint.'

It wasn't, Elizabeth knew, that her mother didn't care for her mother-in-law. But there was a kind of hesitation in her feeling for Gran, like a hiccup before you get out a word.

Elizabeth could hear the hesitation in the way her mother laughed, always a few seconds late, at something odd or comical Gran said. And she could see it when Gran came through the front door of their farmhouse north of Boston at Christmas, carrying her old morocco leather suitcase in one hand and a shopping bag of gifts in the other. Mom would nearly always wait a minute too long to hug her so that Gran, after a brief pause, would walk past her into the living-room. Then she might say something like 'I'm glad to see you haven't blocked up that fireplace yet' or 'I hope you don't pull the shades down on these shorter days. The light is so smoky and mysterious. These folk around here tend to pull down their shades at five p.m., and they'll do it on the last day of the world.'

Elizabeth could see her mother's mouth tighten at the very moment she was trying to smile.

The farmhouse had been Gran's before she'd deeded it over to Elizabeth's father and his family the year she'd moved north. Before that, before Elizabeth had been born, the three of them had lived together while Charles Benedict was finishing law school.

Even though Elizabeth's mother had already begun teaching the fifth grade in a local school and had regular pay cheques, living with Gran had been a financial godsend, Daddy said. There hadn't been much money in those days.

Elizabeth understood how irritating Gran could be, yet she knew that her mother admired her. Elizabeth did, too. Though Gran didn't pay much attention to her as a rule, and she could be sharp.

One Thanksgiving, she'd told Elizabeth that if she described something as *cool* once more, she'd have her arrested for melting down the English language.

'Policemen don't arrest you for that,' Elizabeth responded.

'I'll make a citizen's arrest,' said Gran, and burst into laughter.

That was how it often went between the young Benedicts and the old Benedict. Gran would say something cutting, then smile or laugh outright. But when she was around, there was an edge to the days, a kind of nervy liveliness. Even Elizabeth's father, a rather silent man, would grow talkative, arguing with Gran about painters he thought were better than she did, and about a dozen other things. The hundred-year-old conversation, Elizabeth called it in her mind.

Now and then, on a rainy day, Elizabeth would go up to the attic that Gran had used for a studio when she had lived in the farmhouse. There were two old trunks there, a battered easel near the big north-facing window, and a few canvasses propped against an unfinished wall. Some pencil sketches were still tacked to a rickety screen. One was of Elizabeth as a tiny infant. At times she thought it looked like her, but at other times it could have been any infant in the world.

There was one finished painting among the canvasses. It was a winter landscape. Two crows sat on a fence that slanted across snow-covered corn stubble in a long field that reached to the horizon. Elizabeth liked that painting and told Gran so.

'It looks just like what I see out the window in winter,' she'd said.

'Do you only like what you can recognise?' Gran asked her. She seemed really curious.

'How can I like something I can't recognise?' Elizabeth asked after thinking a moment.

'Why do you have to like everything?' Gran asked.

Elizabeth was speechless.

'I mean,' Gran went on in an unusually gentle voice, 'can't you just be interested in things? And forget about liking?'

She'd brought Elizabeth a small pearl ring one Christmas. She'd found it in a shop on a shabby boulevard in Paris.

'One of those places you can't imagine surviving from one week to another, like some of the little stores you see here in town. The owner had a few rings in the window, a cameo or two, a boring old gold chain, and the ring I got you. The shop was no bigger than a closet, but when I went inside I saw that the walls were covered with photographs of a beautiful chestnut racehorse.

It turned out the man owned that horse. It had won two races for him. Suzerain was its name, and it was what he loved most in the world. He kept the shop to support the horse, not himself. I found he was originally from Algiers. Your little ring is connected to all of that, Elizabeth. Do you know where Algiers is?'

'Sort of,' Elizabeth had replied.

' "Sort of" won't do for geography,' Gran said. So very soon she'd found an atlas in the house and shown Elizabeth just where Algiers was, and told her a few things about colonies and revolutions.

Gran was an encyclopaedia of her own interests.

But she didn't know much about music of any kind. As for books, all Gran read were poetry, or the diaries and letters of painters. She could see why people liked stories, she told Elizabeth, but after a few pages of a novel, she'd find herself dropping the book and going to a window or a door to look out at something, a bird winging its way across the sky, or a tree branch, or even some tourist on the street below her living-room window in Camden, pausing a moment to stare around blankly and scratch his bottom.

What poetry told her, Gran said, was 'about the hidden and true life inside yourself,' about longing and hope and sorrow. In that conversation, Elizabeth had felt oppressed by Gran's words, her intent expression. She'd felt a powerful impulse to shout something rude.

Once, Gran had read to her a few letters a painter named Vincent van Gogh had written to his brother, Theo. It seemed to Elizabeth that they were all about not having any money and needing to buy paints.

'What do you think?' Gran had asked her when she'd finished reading. 'Did you notice that he didn't even mention he was half-starved?'

Elizabeth didn't know what she thought. But she felt a small thrill of pleasure, as she always did when Gran spoke to her that way – as if she could think if only she would.

During these exchanges, Elizabeth didn't feel Gran was paying attention to her so much as she was paying attention to what most concerned her. She never asked Elizabeth about schoolwork or grades, or what she wanted to be when she grew up. Elizabeth had to admit to herself that it was a relief that she didn't.

Yet despite all the things about Gran that made her fun to be with, unpredictable and ungrandmotherly, she was the last person on earth Elizabeth wanted to spend a whole month with.

She knew exactly why she had been sent away. It was because of Stephen Lindsay Benedict, one week old on July 19, her brother, around whose cradle her parents stood as though it held a holy object, and whose raspy kitten cries woke Elizabeth all night long.

Mom and Daddy were old, in their forties. What kind of a thing to do was that – at their age? By the time the baby was as old as Elizabeth, they'd be using walkers.

'We didn't really plan him,' Mom said to Elizabeth, her face rosy and smiling. Elizabeth shuddered. 'But that's life,' Mom said, as she pressed the wrapped-up bundle with the red moony face close to her chest.

When Elizabeth first told her friend, Nancy, that her mother was going to have a baby, she was embarrassed. She could barely get the words out.

Nancy looked grave. 'And they call us irresponsible,' she remarked.

'It's disgusting,' Elizabeth burst out and felt a twinge of guilt.

The worst part of it, now that Stephen Lindsay had arrived to live in the old farmhouse, was a thing she couldn't bear to say out loud. It was that her parents wanted to be alone with the little thing so much that they could hardly wait to get her out of the house.

Then they could eat him all up. Pet him and spoil him. Murmur and croon and smile foolishly while he split the walls with his howls for attention.

The Ghost of Thomas Kempe

PENELOPE LIVELY

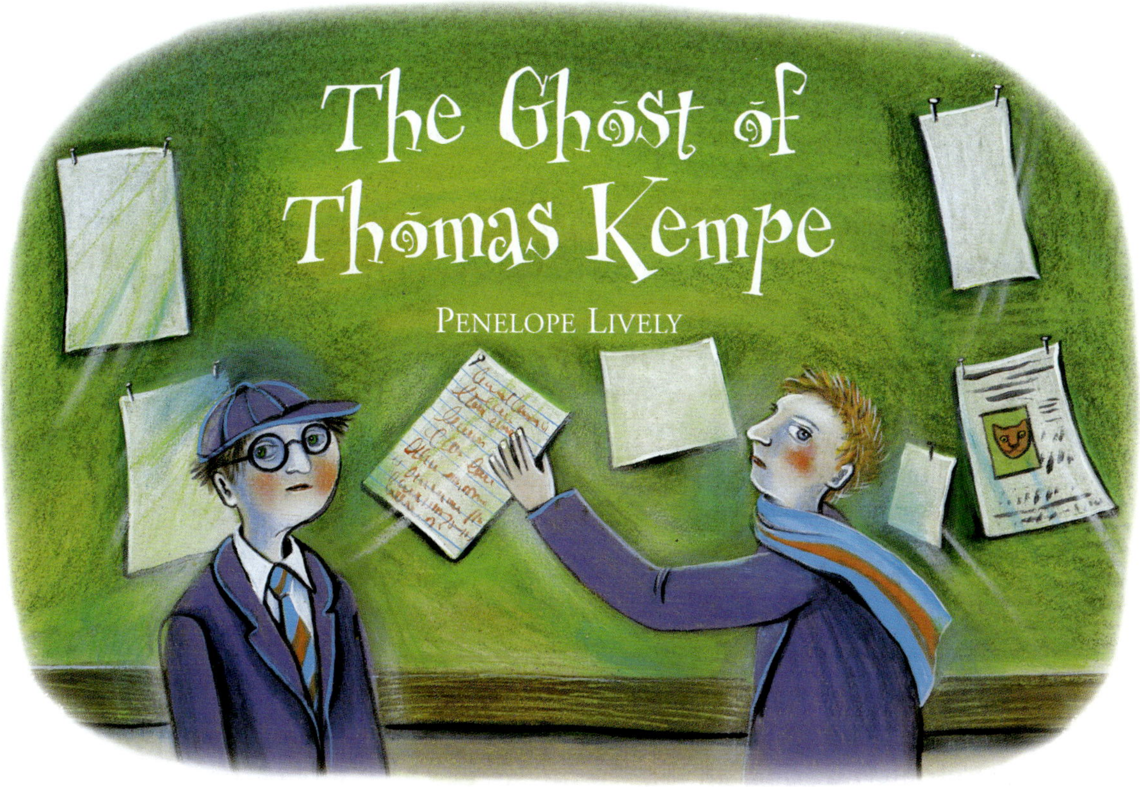

Chapter Three

James and his family have moved to an old house not realising that a ghost lives there too. The ghost seems especially keen to annoy James.

It was tacked to the wooden frame of the notice-board with a rusty nail. Almost before James had read it he knew what was coming. The writing was larger this time, and the letters rather more carefully formed. It was obviously intended to be a notice, or, more precisely, an advertisement. It read:

> ***For the discoverie of goodes loste by the crystalle or by booke and key or with the sieve & sheeres seeke me at my dwellynge which lyes at the extremetie of East Ende Lane. I have muche skille also in such artes as alchemie, astronomie etc. & in physicke & in the seekynge out of wytches & other eville persons. My apprentice, who dwells at the same howse, will bring me messages.***

It was signed, rather flamboyantly, with much swirl and flourish:

> ***Thos. Kempe Esq. Sorcerer.***

'There!' said James, with mixture of triumph and despair. 'There! Now do you believe me?'

Simon took his glasses off, scrubbed round them with his fingers and read the notice for a second time, 'Well,' he said cautiously.

'Well what?'

'Somebody could have put it there.'

'Such as who?'

'I don't know.'

'Such as me, perhaps?' said James in a freezing voice.

'No. Not you. You've been with me all morning. You know something?'

James didn't answer.

'If anyone sees it,' Simon went on amiably, 'they might sort of connect it with you. Because it mentions your house.'

James's anger gave way to alarm. 'What shall I do?'

Simon glanced up and down the street. There was no one in sight. The police-station windows stared blankly down at them.

'Take it off. Quickly.'

James hesitated. Then he darted forward, tweaked the notice from the nail and began to walk quickly away down the road, stuffing it in his pocket. Simon caught him up.

'Let's have another look.'

Pulling the notice out again, James saw with indignation that his own red biro had been used once more, and a page from his exercise book. He tore it into very small pieces and put it in a litter basket by the bus stop.

'Whoever he is, this person,' said Simon, 'he's got some pretty funny ideas, hasn't he? Jiggery-pokery with sieves and whatnot to find out who stole things. He'd make a pretty rotten policemen. And leaves for medicines and all that. It wouldn't work - not now there's penicillin and things.'

'He just wants things done like they were in his time,' said James. 'With him doing them. And me helping.'

'Oh,' said Simon. 'I see.' He sounded very polite. Too polite.

James said, 'You don't believe he's a ghost, do you?'

'I didn't say I didn't.'

'But you don't.'

'I kind of half do and half don't,' said Simon with great honesty. 'I do when I'm with you but I think if I was by myself I wouldn't.'

They walked on for a few minutes in silence. Then Simon said, 'What are you going to do? I mean, whatever it is or whoever it is he keeps getting you into trouble.'

'I know. And I'm getting fed up with it. What *can* I do?'

'If he is - what you think,' said Simon, 'there's one thing you could try.'

'What?'

'Ask him to stop it.'

James stared. 'Talk back to him?'

'That's it. Worth trying anyway.'

'Yes. I s'pose it might be.' Somehow that had not occurred to him. But, when you stopped and thought about it, there was no reason why this should be a one way conversation. If he was here, this Thos. Kempe, Sorcerer, making a right nuisance of himself, then the best thing might well be to talk straight back at him. Maybe that was all that was needed. Just explain quietly and firmly that this sort of thing really wouldn't do, and he'd see reason and go away. Back where he came from, wherever that might be.

Feeling rather more hopeful about the future James parted from Simon at his gate and went home for lunch.

A feeling of dissatisfaction hovered around the house. Mrs Harrison was suffering one of her attacks of hay fever, which made her red-eyed and irritable. Mr Harrison had fallen over a bucket of water standing in the porch, and was resignedly mopping up the mess as James arrived. He followed James into the kitchen, carrying bucket and cloth, which he dumped down by the sink.

'I don't want to interfere with the housekeeping arrangements,' he said, 'but I must point out that the best place for a full bucket of water is not the centre of the front porch.'

'Not guilty,' said his wife, sneezing violently. 'Must have been a child. And don't talk to me about water. I think I'm about to melt as it is.' She began peeling potatoes, with vicious stabs.

'I've only just come in, haven't I?' said James.

'Good gracious!' said Mr Harrison. 'You don't imagine I'd ever suspect it might have been you, do you?' James gave him a suspicious look and went out into the garden to make sure Helen hadn't been interfering with his hole. He found that Tim had located a tributary to the original rat-hole in the drain, and had spent a happy morning digging up a clump of irises. James hastily re-planted them: Tim never seemed to understand that he was only living with them on sufferance as it was and might one day go too far. Mr Harrison had several times said darkly, 'That dog will have to go.'

James patted him kindly. 'You didn't know they weren't weeds, did you?' he said. 'Like you couldn't know Dad still wanted that pair of slippers. Lucky thing I found where you'd buried them, eh?' Tim dropped his head slightly, and bared his teeth in a kind of pink grin, which was the nearest he came to a gesture of affection. He wasn't one of those dogs who climb all over you. He had dignity.

'Come here, sir,' said James sternly. He saw himself and Tim, suddenly, as an intrepid team of criminal-trackers: Harrison of the Yard and his famous trained Rumanian Trufflehound, the Burglar's Scourge. He began to slink along the side of the house with a ferocious scowl on his face, towing a reluctant Tim by the collar. On the other side of that drainpipe lurked the notorious Monte Carlo Diamond Gang, armed to the teeth …

'Lunch!' shouted Mrs Harrison from the scullery window. Tim shook himself free and bolted for the back door.

After lunch the pewter clouds that had been slowly massing above the village all morning opening up into determined, continuous rain. Mrs Harrison said she felt as though she was being drowned from without as well as within, and went to bed with a book. Mr Harrison went to sleep in an armchair. Helen went to see a friend.

James remembered he had some homework to do. He climbed up to his bedroom, closed the door, and sat down at his table. Tim padded round the room once or twice, jumped up on his bed, swirled the covers around several times until he achieved a satisfactory position, and went to sleep. Outside, the rain drummed on the roof and poured in oily rivers down the window.

James opened his project book, looked at his notes, and began to write. It was a project about ancient Greece, and he was enjoying it. He looked things up, and wrote, and stuck some pictures in, and thought about Alexander the Great, and drew a picture of a vase with blokes having a battle on it, and forgot about everything except what he was doing. Around him, the room rustled occasionally: a piece of paper floated to the floor, and a pen rolled across the table. Tim twitched in his sleep.

All of a sudden something nudged James's foot. It was a sheet from his exercise book. He picked it up and read:

> ***I am glad to see thee at thy studies, though I lyke not thy bookes. Where is thy Latin? & where are thy volumes of Astrologie? But to our businesse …***
> ***I have putt out the water for people to knowe wee are seeking thieves: it will doe for a crystalle. Thy father's baldnesse could be stayed by bathing with an ointment made from the leaves of Yarrow (a herb of Venus) but there is no cure for thy mother's ailmente of the eyes for it is caused by wytcherie. Nothing will suffice save to seek out the wytch & bring her to justice. This muste wee doe with all haste.***

James swung round in his chair. Then he got up and searched the room, even looking under the bed. There was nothing to be seen, and nothing moved.

He read the note again. The reference to his father's baldness he found particularly annoying. That was cheek, that was. In fact, he thought, he's a proper busybody, that's what he is.

And then he remembered Simon's suggestion. All right then, let's have a go. Let's try talking to him.

He cleared his throat, feeling distinctly foolish at addressing the empty room, even though there was no one to hear, and said, 'Er – Mr Kempe.'

Silence. Tim uncurled himself and looked up, yawning.

James took a deep breath and said firmly, 'I'm afraid I can't do the things you want me to do because people don't go in much for sorcery nowadays. I don't think they'd really be very interested. You see we don't use those kind of medicines now because we've got penicillin and that and we've got policemen for finding out if anyone's pinched things and catching thieves and my mother gets hay-fever every year and it really isn't anything to do with witchcraft it's because she's allergic to … '

There was a loud crash behind him. He whirled round. One of his clay pots had fallen on to the floor and smashed. Even as he looked, a second one raised itself from the shelf, flew across the room, narrowly missing his right ear, and dashed itself against the opposite wall. Tim leapt from the bed and rushed about the room, barking furiously.

'Hey! Stop that!' shouted James.

A gust of wind swept wildly round the room, lifting all the papers on the table and whirling them about the floor. The ink-bottle scuttered to the edge of the table and hung there till James grabbed hold of it with one hand while with the other he made ineffectual dabs at the flying pages from his project book.

'Here! Lay off! Cut it out!'

The door opened and banged itself shut again, twice. The windows rattled as though assaulted by a sudden thunderstorm. The calendar above the bed reared up, twitched itself from the hook, and flapped to the floor. A glass of water on the bedside table tipped over and broke, making a large puddle on the mat. Downstairs, James could hear the sitting-room door open, and his father's footsteps across the hall.

'Please!' he squeaked breathlessly, using one hand to steady the chair, which was bucking about like a ship in a storm, while with the other he warded off Volume 1 of *A Child's Encyclopaedia* which had risen from the bookshelf and hurled itself at his head.

'Please! Don't! Look, perhaps I could ...'

Mrs Harrison's bedroom door opened and her voice could be heard saying something loud and not very friendly on the landing. Mr Harrison was coming up the stairs.

The bedcover whisked off the bed, whirled round once or twice, and sank to the floor, engulfing a frantic Tim in its folds.

'All right!' shouted James. 'All right! I'll do it. Anything. If you stop.'

The room subsided. Tim struggled out from under the bedcover and dived for the shelter of the bed. The door opened and Mr Harrison came in. James stood amid the wreckage of his room and waited for the storm to break.

The Great Gilly Hopkins

Katherine Paterson

Chapter Two: Welcome to Thompson Park

'Gilly,' said Miss Ellis with a shake of her long blond hair toward the passenger in the back seat. 'I need to feel that you are willing to make some effort.'

Galadriel Hopkins shifted her bubble gum to the front of her mouth and began to blow gently. She blew until she could barely see the shape of the social worker's head through the pink bubble.

'This will be your third home in less than three years.' Miss Ellis swept her golden head left to right and then began to turn the wheel in a cautious manoeuvre to the left. 'I would be the last person to say that it was all your fault. The Dixons' move to Florida, for example. Just one of those unfortunate things. And Mrs Richmond having to go into the hospital' – it seemed to Gilly that there was a long, thoughtful pause before the caseworker went on – 'for her nerves.'

Pop!

Miss Ellis flinched and glanced in the rear-view mirror but continued to talk in her calm, professional voice while Gilly picked at the bits of gum stuck in her straggly bangs and on her cheeks and chin. 'We should have been more alert to her condition before placing any foster child there. *I* should have been more alert.'

Cripes, thought Gilly. The woman was getting sincere. What a pain. 'I'm not trying to *blame* you, Gilly. It's just that I need, we all need, your cooperation if any kind of arrangement is to work out.' Another pause. 'I can't imagine you *enjoy* all this moving around.' The blue eyes in the mirror were checking out Gilly's response. 'Now this new foster mother is very different from Mrs Nevins.' Gilly calmly pinched a blob of gum off the end of her nose. There was no use trying to get the gum out of her hair. She sat back and tried to chew the bit she had managed to salvage. It stuck to her teeth in a thin layer. She fished another ball of gum from her jeans pocket and scraped the lint off with her thumbnail before elaborately popping it into her mouth.

'Will you do me a favour, Gilly? Try to get off on the right foot?'

Gilly had a vision of herself sailing around the living room of the foster home on her right foot like an ice skater. With her uplifted left foot she was shoving the next foster mother square in the mouth. She smacked her new supply of gum in satisfaction.

'Do me another favour, will you?' Get rid of that bubble gum before we get there?'

Gilly obligingly took the gum out of her mouth while Miss Ellis's eyes were still in the mirror. Then when the social worker turned her attention back to the traffic, Gilly carefully spread the gum under the handle of the left-hand door as a sticky surprise for the next person who might try to open it.

Two traffic lights farther on Miss Ellis handed back a towelette. 'Here,' she said, see what you can do about that guck on your face before we get there.'

Gilly swiped the little wet paper across her mouth and dropped it on the floor.

'Gilly – ' Miss Ellis sighed and shifted her fancy on-the-floor gears. 'Gilly – '

'My name,' Gilly said between her teeth, 'is Galadriel.'

Miss Ellis appeared not to have heard. 'Gilly, give Maime Trotter half a chance, OK? She's really a nice person.'

That cans it, thought Gilly. At least nobody had accused Mr or Mrs Nevins, her most recent foster parents, of being 'nice'. Mrs Richmond, the one with the bad nerves, had been 'nice'. The Newman family, who couldn't keep a five-year-old who wet her bed, had been 'nice'. Well, I'm eleven now, folks, and, in case you haven't heard, I don't wet my bed anymore. But I am not nice. I am brilliant. I am famous across this entire country. Nobody wants to tangle with the great Galadriel Hopkins. I am too clever and too hard to manage. Gruesome Gilly, they call me. She leaned back comfortably. Here I come, Maime baby, ready or not.

They had reached a neighbourhood of huge trees and old houses. The social worker slowed and stopped beside a dirty white fence. The house it penned was old and brown with a porch that gave it a sort of potbelly.

Standing on the porch, before she rang the bell, Miss Ellis took out a comb. 'Would you try to pull this through your hair?'

Gilly shook her head. 'Can't.'

'Oh, come on, Gilly – '

'No. Can't comb my hair. I'm going for the Guinness Record for uncombed hair.'

'Gilly, for pete's sake … '

'Hey, there, I thought I heard y'all pull up.' The door had opened, and a huge hippopotamus of a woman was filling the doorway. 'Welcome to Thompson Park, Gilly, honey.'

'Galadriel,' muttered Gilly, not that she expected this bale of blubber to manage her real name. Jeez, they didn't have to put her in with a freak.

Half a small face, topped with muddy brown hair and masked with thick metal-rimmed glasses, jutted out from behind Mrs Trotter's mammoth hip.

The woman looked down. 'Well, 'scuse me, honey.' She put her arm around the head as if to draw it forward, but the head resisted movement. 'You want to meet your new sister, don't you? Gilly, this is William Ernest Teague.'

The head immediately disappeared behind Mrs Trotter's bulk. She didn't seem bothered. 'Come in, come in. I don't mean to leave you standing on the porch like you was trying to sell me something. You belong here now.' She backed up. Gilly could feel Miss Ellis's fingers on her backbone gently prodding her through the doorway and into the house.

Inside, it was dark and crammed with junk. Everything seemed to need dusting.

'William Ernest, honey, you want to show Gilly where her room is?'

William Ernest clung to the back of Mrs Trotter's flowered housedress, shaking his head.

'Oh, well, we can see to that later.' She led them down the hallway to a living room. 'Just sit down and make yourself at home, now.' She smiled all across her face at Gilly, like the 'After' in a magazine diet ad – a 'Before' body with an 'After' smile.

The couch was brown and squat with a pile of cushions covered in greying lace at the far end. A matching brown chair with worn arms slumped at the opposite side of the room. Grey lace curtains hung at the single window between them, and beside the window was a black table supporting an old-time TV set with rabbit ears. The Nevinses had had colour TV. On the right-hand wall between the door and the brown chair stood a black upright piano with a dusty brown bench. Gilly took one of the pillows off the couch and used it to wipe every trace of dust off the piano bench before sitting down on it.

From the brown chair Miss Ellis was staring at her with a very nonprofessional glare. Mrs Trotter was lowering herself to the sofa and chuckling. 'Well, we been needing somebody to rearrange the dust around here. Ain't we, William Ernest, honey?'

William Ernest climbed up behind the huge woman and lay behind her back like a bolster pillow, poking his head around from time to time to sneak another look at Gilly.

She waited until Mrs Trotter and Miss Ellis were talking, then gave little W.E. the most fearful face in all her repertory of scary looks, sort of a cross betweeen Count Dracula and Godzilla. The little muddy head disappeared faster than a toothpaste cap down a sink drain.

She giggled despite herself. Both of the women turned to look at her. She switched easily and immediately to her 'Who, me?' look.

Miss Ellis stood up.

'I need to be getting back to the office, Mrs Trotter. You'll let me know' – she turned to Gilly with prickles in her big blue eyes – 'you'll let me know if there're any problems?'

Gilly favoured Miss Ellis with her best barracuda smile.

Meantime Mrs Trotter was laboriously hefting herself to her feet.

'Don't worry, Miz Ellis. Gilly and William Ernest and me is nearly friends already. My Melvin, God rest him, used to say that Trotter never met a stranger. And if he'd said kid, he woulda been right. I never met a kid I couldn't make friends with.'

Gilly hadn't learned yet how to vomit at will, but if she had, she would have dearly loved to throw up on that one. So, lacking the truly perfect response, she lifted her legs and spun around to the piano, where she proceeded to bang out 'Heart and Soul' with her left hand and 'Chop-sticks' with her right.

William Ernest scrambled off the couch after the two women, and Gilly was left alone with the dust, the out-of-tune piano, and the satisfaction that she had indeed started off on the right foot in her new foster home. She could stand anything, she thought – a gross guardian, a freaky kid, an ugly, dirty house – as long as she was in charge.

She was well on the way.

A Christmas Card

PAUL THEROUX

Chapter One

Whenever I see light feathers of snow moving slowly down a window to make a white pillow on the sill, and hear the thin moan of wind through casement cracks in a room where a fireplace is singing with flames, I remember the Christmas when I was nine, and our house at Indian Willows.

We were lost. I knew that from the cold sound of my father's voice. He was angry, he shouted at me and then at my little brother, Louis. If he had known where he was he would have been confident and joked with us. We were in the family car, driving deep into the country. When the first snow started to fall and the car swerved on the icy road, Father hunched over the wheel and growled. The land was white and the sky dark. It was as if we were crossing a harbour at twilight. I was worried – because he was. I did not know what I could do to cheer him up. And the cold in the car's back seat made my fear worse.

It should not have been a desperate trip. Christmas was three days away. We were going to the house for the first time. My father, who was a traveller, had just returned from a journey in Asia.

We had been delighted to see him, and for the early part of this trip to the country he had kept us entranced with stories of things he had seen – snake charmers, elephants trained to beg for rupees, and dancing bears. He had heard of a monkey which always travelled with a tiger, because the tiger was blind and needed the monkey to guide him. They were magical stories, and I felt that Father was touched with the same magic. The stories filled us with a longing to see such things, for it seemed that you had to travel across the world, through a wilderness of snow and fire, to know such enchantments – temples of gold, firewalkers and soothsayers, people vanishing in a puff of smoke.

Father denied this. 'You don't have to go all that way to know what magic is,' he said. As he spoke it began to snow. He smiled and said, 'What is magic? It is something being proven, not necessarily to make you understand, but so you believe. The trick itself is a command, and the command is always the magician saying, "Believe in me!"'

We watched the snow falling. It gave the wind a billowing shape, like sheeted ghosts blowing towards us on the road.

'There is magic everywhere,' said Father.

'At our house?' asked Louis.

'Everywhere,' said Father. He tapped the side of his head with his finger, 'But it's mostly here.'

The house at Indian Willows was Father's surprise. He said it was his present to us for having waited so patiently for him to return. He had shown us a picture of it, taken on a sunny day in summer: a great barn-like building facing the ocean.

I examined the snapshot. 'Are there children there?'

'No neighbours,' he said proudly. 'Not a single one! It's miles from anywhere.'

I was sad. I had hoped there would be other children to play with. And so, even before we left our warm apartment in the city, I dreaded the vast wooden house with the dark windows and the green rooster on the weathervane. I didn't want to go, especially now, at Christmas, leaving everything behind. But Father insisted we would like the house. 'It has a fireplace,' he said. 'It's a huge old-fashioned one. We can chop some logs and build an enormous fire – '

It was the one image in my mind that gave me hope, the flaming logs in the stone hearth of the house at Indian Willows. I saw us gathered around this fire on a snowy night, until the image represented everything that Christmas was – light and joy. The fire assumed different shapes, changing from a bunch of plumes, to a sunrise, and then to a brilliant animal. To live in a house with a living fire – it was like having a tiger crouched in the wall of your room, yawning and flickering and blazing like a god.

We left the city on a cold morning. It was so early the street lights were still on, solitary yellow beacons in the empty avenues. We drove through the darkness like people escaping. We had brought a picnic lunch, which we ate in the parked car at the roadside, and all through lunch Father had studied a map while Mother fed us sandwiches. Later in the afternoon, on a narrow road (Father talking about magic), the snow began – first a flurry, then clouds of small sweeping flakes. With the snow it grew dark. The houses and stores we passed were shut, their windows unlighted, like blind eyes.

I said, 'Can we stop and buy something?'

I did not want to buy anything. I wanted to know why those buildings were deserted.

'Impossible. They're only open in the summer,' said Father.

Summer seemed so distant. The long drive and the winter cold were making me feel sick. I envied Louis, who was fast asleep and snoring, with his hands in his pockets.

'Why – ?' I started to say. It was then that Father shouted at us to be quiet. Mother reached back and stroked my hair. I knew that Father was lost. This made him seem angry, but really he was worried.

'There's a hotel,' said Mother.

'Closed for the winter,' said Father, and he swore. He did it forcefully, spitting out the words he told us we should never say.

The car slowed down. Ahead, through the snow tumbling in the headlights, I saw a fork in the road.

Mother rattled the map. She said, 'I can't figure this out.'

'Go left,' I said.

Father turned around and said, 'Why?'

The road on the left was wider. It had tyre marks and telephone poles and a very secure fence. It looked safe. But I did not know how to explain this. On wide roads I felt as if we were heading home, on narrower ones I doubted that we would ever arrive, and there were some small roads on which I felt we would disappear - just ahead - where the road seemed to end.

I said, 'Because there are signs on that one.'

'We've been driving for hours,' said Mother.

'I think Marcel has a point - about those signs,' said Father. He took the left fork. The snow was deep on this new road, and it was still falling. We were travelling down a tunnel that was white and collapsing softly upon us. The car slipped sideways and Father cursed. I was too afraid to move and warm myself. I prayed that we would arrive soon.

I had always trusted Father. He was funny, he was strong, he had made long and difficult journeys. But today he seemed different, somewhat confused by the snowstorm and uncertain of the road.

A storm to me then was simply terror and unusual noises. It was the pain in my toes from the aching cold, the stale smell of the car; it was delay. I was car-sick, I was impatient, I was sorry we had come. I had not really known why I had not wanted to leave home. Now I knew. The snow was relentless - it blocked the windows and made the wipers spank the frames. It was the reason we were alone on the road. We should not be here, I thought. This snow, these woods, this wobbling ride - it might never end.

And there was something else that I was almost too fearful to think: that my father - as reckless as he was brave - was doing something foolishly wrong, that he was misbehaving or breaking some law. He knew better than to lead us through this storm. But he had sneaked us away from home and now he was lost and so we were all lost.

Mother said, 'It's so dark - do you think we have far to go?'

'Ask Marcel,' said Father sharply. 'He's the one who told me to take a left.'

'Don't be childish,' said Mother. She often said this to him when he upset her.

'It's not far,' I said. I saw birds huddled in the trees at the roadside, roosting in the branches. This frightened me - even birds knew better than to travel in a snowstorm. And under each dark tree was a darker thing, like a panther, a sleek humpbacked shadow with its wicked face lowered in the snow, watching us pass.

'Look,' said Louis, waking and yawning, 'a light. Is that our house?'

'No,' said Father. 'But let's stop and get directions.'

The light flickered like fire.

'What is the light doing?' asked Louis.

Father was silent. He eased the car off the road into the driveway of a house so tall it rose like a chimney, upwards into the stormy night. The snow appeared to fall from its upper storeys. It had a porch and an empty trellis, but its narrow windows glowed brightly and the light, as much a warning as a welcome, made it stranger than if it had been in total darkness.

Mother said, 'Is it a hotel?'

'It looks that way,' said Father. 'I can't imagine why it's still open. Maybe there's someone inside who knows where we are.'

He turned off the engine and walked towards the house through the troughs of snow. And he vanished inside.

Me and Nu: Childhood at Coole

ANNE GREGORY

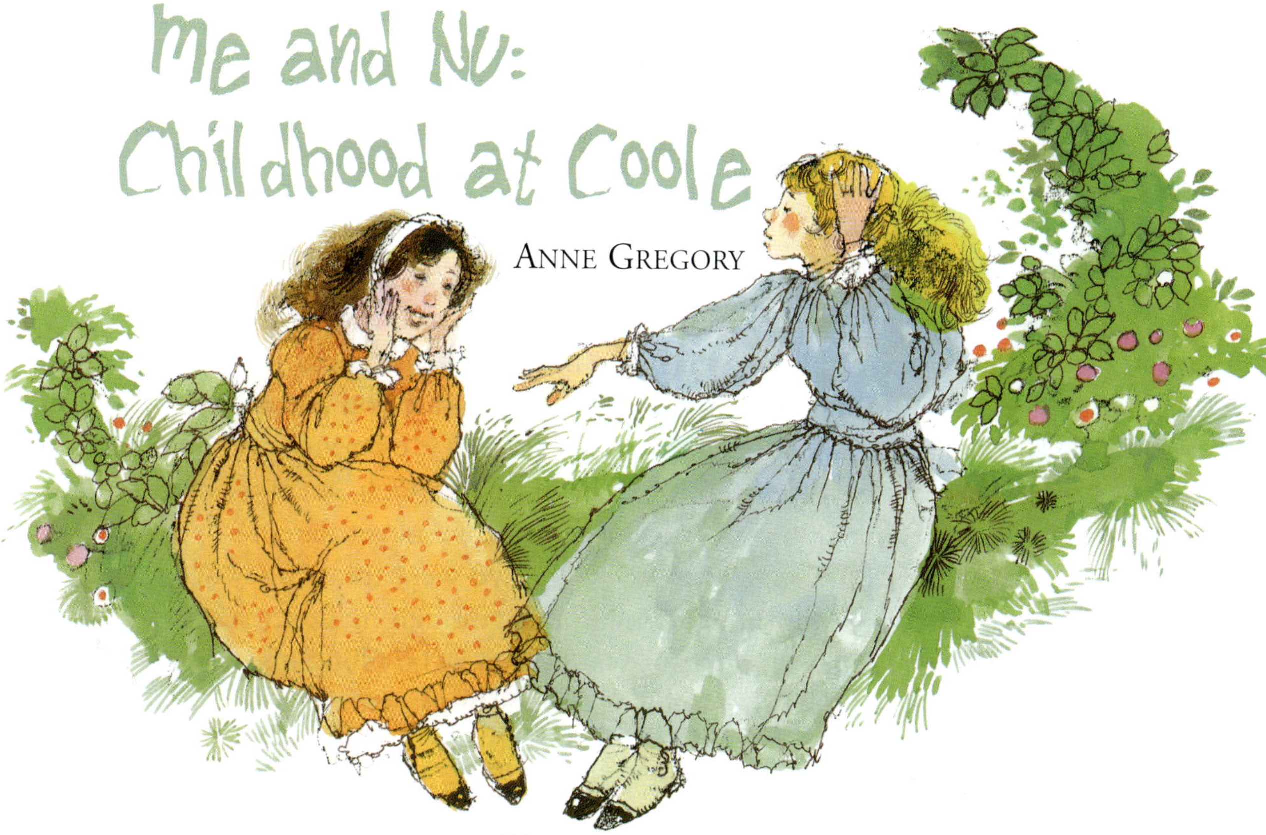

Chapter Five

Many of the great Irish literary figures of the 20th century, including W.B. Yeats and Sean O'Casey, spent time at Coole Park – Lady Gregory's estate in Galway. Me and Nu *is written by one of her grandchildren, Anne and gives an interesting insight into Lady Gregory's house guests.*

Mr Yeats used to stay with us at Coole from as far back as I can remember.

There was a large bed of sedum in the flower garden, by the first vinery; in the summer it was alive with butterflies and I can remember Mamma once saying that sedum flowered all summer; and while it was in flower Yeats would be at Coole.

He always seemed to be there, leaning back in his chair at table – huge, with (in our eyes) an enormous tummy. He wore a signet ring with an enormous stone in it on his little finger, and Nu and I used to giggle like mad, and say he expected everyone to kiss it, like the Pope. She and I used to copy his habit of running his fingers through the great lock of hair that fell forward over his forehead, and then hold out our hand with the imaginary ring, saying: 'This ring is a holy ring; it has been in touch with my holy halo.'

We all lunched and had tea together. Nu and I didn't dine with the grown-ups, but Richard sometimes did.

Marian always waited at table at dinner, and Richard told us that Mr Yeats always sat with his chair pushed back much farther from the table than anyone else, and every time Marian passed behind him, she used to kick the back leg of his chair, by accident on purpose, and then say, 'I'm sorry Sir, I never saw you had pulled back from the table.' Richard said Marian did it over and over again, and Mr Yeats never moved his chair in by one inch. Nu and I dared each other to kick his chair leg at tea, but we never dared.

Mr Yeats didn't speak much – while we were there anyway – and seemed sunk in thought, miles away, though he never seemed to miss any food. Grandma always seemed to be filling his cup, which he passed up the moment it was empty, without looking up and without a word.

'Manners' Nu and I used to signal to each other with a disapproving look: 'did you see? No please or thank you.'

We had tea outside the front door on the gravel sweep every day in the summer and it never rained.

Mr Yeats sat on the garden chair that had wooden arms and a high back. Grandma sat on the green painted garden seat with curled iron arms and a back that curved over backwards, and we children had wicker stools with four legs, made by the travelling basket maker. They were made from withies and dogwood that grew on the side of the avenue. Yellow willow and red dogwood, and they had very comfortable slightly concave circular seats, and were just the right height for the tables. The tables were really just pieces of polished mahogany that folded in half. Marian and Ellen used to carry them out and put them on low trestles, and then Marian carried the enormous silver tray with the silver teapot with the acorn on the lid, and the enormous silver hot water jug, and then all the food. Masses of scones and butter and honey and strawberry jam bottled by Grandma, and lots of sponge cakes that Mary made, and which never tasted so heavenly as in the sun.

Mr Yeats actually seemed to talk more when he had tea out of doors, though he still passed his cup without a word, and anyway we often had visitors for tea in the summer.

It was great fun when people came to tea, when we were having it out of doors, because they had to drive up to the front door, virtually up to the tea table. The horses or ponies were taken down to the yard to be looked after by John Diveney, but later there were motor cars, and they merely passed the house, and parked under the enormous Ilex just beyond.

The workmen's bell was fixed in this tree, and was rung at 8.00 a.m., 12.00 noon, 1.00 p.m. and 6.00 p.m. for the starting and stopping of work. It was a lovely bell but woe betide any of us if we rang it at any other hour; though sometimes if Grandma wanted someone from the yard or garden she would tell us to go and give the bell 'two swings only,' which was a thrill.

You could hear the bell nearly three miles away, and the 12 o'clock bellringing meant that however hard pressed Nu and I were, even if our camp was surrounded by Indians, we had to make a determined effort and break out within a few minutes or we'd be late for lunch.

This was one of the few unbreakable rules. We had to be back in the house in time to wash our hands and get tidy before the gong went for lunch, and I cannot remember that we were ever late.

When the Indians were becoming less dangerous - I think we had driven them off so often that they were less anxious to attack - we began to turn our minds to decorating and beautiful houses.

Near the house, on the way down to the flower garden, there was a wonderful place where old laurels had grown into an archway, making a natural entrance to a cave of dark green inside. The removal of a lot of dead wood was fairly easy, and the result was fantastic. A room big enough to carry in a bench and an enormous case that we found in the Haggart. It was easy to find an old table cloth, and we managed to slip out a bedspread for the 'sofa', and we spent several admiring hours here.

However, to have a beautiful interior is not enough. It's all right if the outside has to be disguised to prevent the enemy locating you, but *this* house was for show. It was on the edge of the direct route Grandma or any visitor took from the house to the flower garden, and therefore it must look beautiful and intriguing from the path.

I had a passion for laburnum. I could think of nothing more beautiful than waking in the morning with laburnum growing across my bedroom window in great masses, with the sun shining golden through the flowers on to my bed. So here was my first real chance. I picked a lot of large branches of laburnum covered in tight buds, and planted them either side of the entrance to our mansion.

Then we decided that a mansion must have an avenue - with daffodils. The daffs were out, so we dug up a great number in the woods and planted an avenue of them up to the front door. The ground was very hard and we had great difficulty in making the holes deep enough to cover the bulbs, but we propped the flowers up with sticks, certain that in the morning they would have righted themselves and be standing high and firm. This was perhaps one of the worst disappointments we had known.

It was such a wonderful thing we had planned - the whole rather dark place, glowing with yellow daffodils followed by hanging lanterns of golden laburnum.

Next morning we rushed down to see our lovely house. It was shocking. We could see at once that the laburnum had wilted and was collapsed on the floor - lifeless. That was bad enough, but where were the daffodils? Had they been eaten or what? They'd vanished.

Very slowly we approached, wondering if some horrible animal would rise from the ground, perhaps still chewing the final flower.

And then we saw a few pathetic yellow forms lying on the ground, their colour nearly gone, and looking so tiny and so *few*. Surely we'd planted ten times that number?

It was awful!

It was awful that it *looked* so awful, and it was awful that we had moved the daffs and they were dead, and we had killed them, and it was awful that now no-one would come and admire our new house. I don't think that I have ever been so completely miserable.

Sean O'Casey was staying with us at this time, and he wandered past, gazing at the trees as he seemed to do a great deal of the time. He didn't know the names of the different trees and Grandma was teaching him. He had funny pink eyes and he saw us – or even probably heard us sobbing.

'What's up with you,' he asked us kindly enough, 'have you hurt yourselves?'

'No,' we tried to be grown-up. 'No, we've had trouble with our avenue. The daffodils don't like being divided like this. They were all together, and we think they're *lonely*.' This was invented on the spur of the moment, but we suddenly thought it might be true.

'Ah well,' said Mr O'Casey, 'don't waste your time on lonely daffodils, there's plenty more would welcome your tears.'

We were sure he said this. It sounded very silly to us. Who would want our tears more than our poor dead daffs, killed by our own hands. Before we got too soaked with tears Grandma came along with our elevenses. Dear, dear, Grandma. One glance at the shambles.

'Goodness,' she said, 'what a wonderful idea making an avenue like that. It will be *so* beautiful next year – like a fairy road and if you are at school I'll see them coming up and I'll be able to write to you both and tell you about them, and it will make me think of you both every time I go to the flower garden.'

'But Grandma,' we wailed, 'they're dead. We've killed them.'

'Nonsense,' said Grandma, 'they're not *dead*. They may be sulking because they were having a party when you dug them up; but next year they will come up again as bright as buttons. You can never really dig up a flower when it is open and cheerful and obviously having a good time. It resents it. But when it's faded you can, because then it rather likes the idea of going somewhere new,' and Grandma came into our house with our elevenses and sat on the sofa and didn't ask where we'd got the bedspread from.

Thunder and Lightnings

JAN MARK

Chapter Four: Victor

Andrew has moved house and has just started in a new school. This extract begins on the Friday morning of his first week.

On Friday morning Andrew arrived early for the lesson and stationed himself by the teacher's desk, determined to get some information before he did anything else. While he was waiting, he looked round the room to see if there were any survivors from the last lesson and decided that there were at least three people that he had seen before: Jeanette Butler, the boy in the pink shirt and another boy whose appearance worried Andrew because he was sure there was something wrong with him. He was hideously swollen about the body but very thin in the face. Andrew leaned against the desk and wondered what kind of disease could possibly cause a person to become such a horrid shape. The boy's spindly legs seemed hardly strong enough to support the rest of him.

'You're the new boy, are you?' said someone beside him. 'I'm Miss Beale, who are you?'

'I'm Mitchell,' said Andrew. 'Andrew Mitchell, Miss.' It sounded like a silly sort of tongue twister.

'How do you like it here?' said Miss Beale. Andrew didn't intend to be side-tracked.

'What are we supposed to be doing?' he asked.

'That rather depends on you,' said Miss Beale. 'In General Studies you can choose your own subject and follow it through. You'll be rather behind the others but you can start on a project now and work on it through the holidays. That's what most of the others will do, if they haven't finished by next week.'

Andrew found this hard to believe.

'What are you interested in?' asked Miss Beale.

'Motor racing, guinea-pigs,' said Andrew.

'Well, either of those would do for a start,' said Miss Beale. 'Perhaps Victor would show you round so that you can see how the others set about it.' Andrew thought she wanted to be rid of him and when he turned round he found that a restive queue had formed behind him. Miss Beale directed him to Victor. He was the very fat boy with the very thin face.

Andrew was reluctant to go any closer. How could he stroll up and hold a normal conversation with anyone so deformed? He picked up his satchel and walked casually round the fat boy's desk as though he just happened to be passing it. When he got close, Andrew realised that Victor was not fat at all. On the contrary, he was exceptionally thin; all of him, not just his head and legs. The fat part was made up of clothes. Andrew could see a white T-shirt, a red shirt, a blue sweater and a red sweater. Further down he wore a pair of black jeans with orange patches sewn over the knees and yellow patches on the hip pockets. Over it all he had an anorak so covered in badges and buttons that it was difficult to tell what colour it was.

In fact, he was not so much dressed as camouflaged. Even his hair seemed to be some part of a disguise, more like a wig than live hair, dusty black as if it had been kicked round the floor before being put on. It was so long at the front that Victor was actually looking through it. His ears stuck out cheerfully, like a Radar device.

'Miss Beale said you would show me round, to look at the projects,' said Andrew.

'Why, do you want to copy one?' asked Victor, lifting a strand of hair and exposing one eye. 'You could copy mine, only someone might recognise it. I've done that three times already.'

'Whatever for?' said Andrew. 'Don't you get tired of it?'

Victor shook his head and his hair.

'That's only once a year. I did that two times at the junior school and now I'm doing that again,' he said. 'I do fish, every time. Fish are easy. They're all the same shape.'

'No, they're not,' said Andrew.

'They are when I do them,' said Victor. He spun his book round, with one finger, to show Andrew the drawings. His fish were not only all the same shape, they were all the same shape as slugs. Underneath each drawing was a printed heading: BRAEM; TENSH; CARP; STIKLBAK; SHARK. It was the only way of telling them apart. The shark and the bream were identical, except that the shark had a row of teeth like tank traps.

'Isn't there a "c" in stickleback?' said Andrew. Victor looked at his work.

'You're right.' He crossed out both 'k's, substituted 'c's and pushed the book away, the better to study it. 'I got that wrong last year.'

Andrew flipped over a few pages. There were more slugs: PLACE; COD; SAWFISH; and a stringy thing with a frill round its neck: EEL.

'Don't you have to write anything?' asked Andrew.

'Yes, look. I wrote a bit back here. About every four pages will do,' said Victor. 'Miss Beale, she keep saying I ought to write more but she's glad when I don't. She's got to read it. Nobody can read my writing.'

Andrew was not surprised. Victor's writing was a sort of code to deceive the enemy, with punctuation marks in unlikely places to confuse anyone who came too close to cracking the code. He watched Andrew counting the full stops in one sentence and said, 'I put those in while I think about the next word. I like doing question marks better.' He pointed out two or three specimens, independent question marks, without questions. They looked like curled feathers out of a pillow. One had a face.

'Do you put a question mark in every sentence?' said Andrew.

'Oh yes. I know you don't actually need them,' said Victor, 'but they're nice to do.'

Andrew turned to the last page of the book. There was a drawing of a whale.

'Whales aren't fish,' said Andrew.

'Aren't they?' said Victor. 'Are you sure? I always put a whale in.'

'Whales are mammals.'

'What's a mammal?' said Victor. He wrote 'This.is.not.a.fish?' under his whale and closed the book. 'Come and see the others.'

'Mammals don't lay eggs,' said Andrew, as they set off round the room.

'That's a pity,' said Victor. 'I'd like to see a whale's egg. Big as a bath, wouldn't that be?' He stopped by the boy in the pink shirt. 'Let's have a look at your project, Tim.'

Andrew thought he had seen most of Tim's project before. It featured a man in a tree, knotty with muscles and wearing a leopard skin.

'Tarzan,' said Tim.

'Why do a project about Tarzan?' said Andrew.

'Tarzan's easy,' said Tim. 'You just cut him out and stick him in.'

'Fish are easier,' said Victor.

'Why not do worms then?' said Andrew. 'Nothing could be easier than worms. Wiggle-wiggle-wiggle: all over in a second. Page one, worms are long and thin. Page two, worms are round.'

Victor began to grin but Tim sat down to give the idea serious consideration.

Victor's grin became wider, revealing teeth like Stonehenge.

'I reckon you're catching on,' he said. 'Why don't you do worms?'

'I want to do something interesting,' said Andrew.

'Ho,' said Victor. 'You'll come to a bad end, you will.'

They went on around the room. Andrew noticed that nearly all the boys were doing a project on fish or fishing. The girls tended to specialise in horses except for Jeannette Butler, who wouldn't let them see hers.

'Why don't you go and stand in the road and catch cars?' said Jeannette, giving them a hefty shove when they tried to look.

'Give us a kiss,' said Victor and got a poke in the chest instead.

'I think I'll do motor racing,' said Andrew when they got back to Victor's desk. 'I know a bit about that, already. Me and my Dad used to go to Brand's Hatch a lot, when we lived in Kent.'

'Where's Kent?' said Victor. 'Down at the bottom somewhere, isn't it?'

'Some of it is,' said Andrew. 'We were further up, near London.' Andrew fetched a piece of drawing paper and sat down to draw a Formula One racing car. Victor drew some scales on his whale and broadcast punctuation marks throughout the book, letting them fall wherever he fancied.

At the end of the lesson the group split up again. Andrew thought he had seen the last of Victor who elbowed his way out of the room and was lost from sight in the roaring mob that boiled towards the canteen. Andrew followed on his own, consumed with disappointment. During the lesson it had seemed as though he might have found a friend. He wondered if he had offended Victor, by telling him how to spell stickleback, and that whales weren't fish. He would have done better to keep his information to himself. If Victor had told him that his racing car had oval wheels he felt sure that he would have been offended, even though it was true.

All through the lunch hour he kept a look-out, hoping to catch sight of Victor's grin in the distance, but as usual he ended up walking round the playground by himself.

When school was over he began to walk home alone. Once out of town there was no pavement on the Pallingham road so he climbed the bank and teetered dangerously along the top of it, his feet on a level with the roofs of passing cars. After a few minutes he felt someone punch his foot, and looking down he saw Victor drawing alongside on a bicycle with handlebars that rose so high in the air that Victor seemed to be dangling from them. Andrew slithered down the bank to the road and Victor scooted along beside him.

'Do you live out this way then?' said Victor.

'In Pallingham, yes,' said Andrew. 'We moved in last week.'

'You don't live in the Newmans' old place, do you?' asked Victor. 'Tiler's Cottage, back of the church?'

'That's it,' said Andrew.

'Well then, you're our next door neighbours, almost. We live down the loke.'

'Down the what?'

'Down the loke.'

'What's a loke?'

Victor looked puzzled. 'A loke's a loke. Don't you have lokes in Kent?'

'No, we don't. What is it, a hole?'

'How can that be a hole?' asked Victor.

'You said you lived down one,' said Andrew. Victor pointed across the road at a gap between two houses. 'That's a loke.' Andrew looked.

'It's a lane.'

'That's not. Lanes go somewhere, lokes stop halfway. I'll show you our loke when we get home. Fancy us being neighbours. What did you want to move up here for and come to our rotten old school?'

'What's rotten about it?' said Andrew. 'I've seen worse.'

'I hate school,' said Victor. 'No, I don't. I don't hate that. I just wish that was different.'

'You wouldn't wish it was like my last school,' said Andrew. 'I hated that. There was too many of us. I met our house master in the street one day and he didn't recognise me and that was after a whole term.'

'Everyone recognise me,' said Victor. 'Haven't you heard them? "Is that you at the back, Skelton? Stop talking, Skelton. Come you out of that toilet, Skelton." '

'Who's Skelton?'

'Me,' said Victor.

'At my other school half the teachers never knew our names,' said Andrew. 'I got caught down the boiler room one day and I was so scared I gave a false name. This teacher said "What's your name, lad?" and I said Graham Hill. It was the first name I could think of. I'd seen him the night before, on the television.'

'Did that teacher find out?'

'No; but there was another Graham Hill in the second year. He found out,' said Andrew, remembering what the other Graham Hill had done about it.

'I bet he was pleased,' said Victor. 'I bet he was. What were you doing in the boiler room?'

'It was better than going on the playground,' said Andrew. 'Everybody was in a gang. I wasn't in a gang. They said I talked stuck-up.'

'They must have talked horrible if you sounded stuck-up,' said Victor frankly.

'I didn't realise then,' said Andrew, 'that you have to talk different at school than you do at home.'

'I don't,' said Victor. 'I swear a bit more at school than I do at home, but I reckon I sound the same, doing it.'

'Then I started talking at home like I did at school. I didn't notice but my Mum did. She didn't think much of it, I can tell you. I think that's one of the reason we moved.'

'You never moved because of the way you were talking,' said Victor.

'It wasn't only that. Just after my brother was born Mum held him up and said, "He looks like a teeny weeny soccer hooligan already. It must be in the air, let's move." So we did.'

'Is he a soccer hooligan?' asked Victor, with interest. 'Boots and that?'

'Of course he isn't, he's only eight months old,' said Andrew. 'Mum never says what she means. She says something different and you have to guess. We've moved seven times since I was born. I went to three junior schools and two secondary schools. This is the second.'

'Do you think you'll stop, this time?' said Victor.

'We might,' said Andrew. 'Mum and Dad like it here. I expect I shall, in the end.'

'I've always lived here,' said Victor. 'I wish I could go to a different school every term. I wouldn't get bored then.'

'You'd never learn anything.'

'I never learn anything anyway,' said Victor. 'Everybody read better than me. Everybody write better than me. I'd like to join the Airforce when I leave school, but I don't reckon they'd have me. Maybe I'll drive a tractor, like my Dad. What do your Dad do?'

'I don't know, quite,' said Andrew. 'He works with computers. We've got all this paper tape at home, full of holes. It looks as though you ought be able to do something with it but I can never think of anything. Mum made paper chains out of it, last Christmas.'

'Do your Mum work?'

'She used to,' said Andrew. 'She stopped when she had my brother: now she says she'd like to go back, just for the rest. She worked in a library.'

'Books and that? Is she clever then?' asked Victor, suggesting both admiration and disgust.

'Books? You should see our house,' said Andrew. 'We've got thousands, all over the place. I'll tell you, when we move, the first thing that gets unpacked is the books. Then Mum starts reading them and nothing else gets unpacked. We came here a week ago and we haven't even got the curtains up yet. All the books are out though, all over the floor. You can't move.'

'We've got some books,' said Victor. 'Three or four. Do you like reading?'

'Sometimes,' said Andrew. 'Technical manuals and magazines. I don't like reading books unless they're funny.'

'I read so slow I can't tell what's funny and what isn't,' said Victor.

When they reached the church Victor stopped.

'There's a short cut here, round the back. I don't usually use that when I've got the bike but if you give me a hand over the wall we'll go that way.'

They went through the churchyard the way Andrew had gone on his first morning, but instead of using the gate on the far side, Victor led the way round behind the yew trees to a place where the graves were so old and mossy they were sinking back into the ground. Victor sat himself astride the wall.

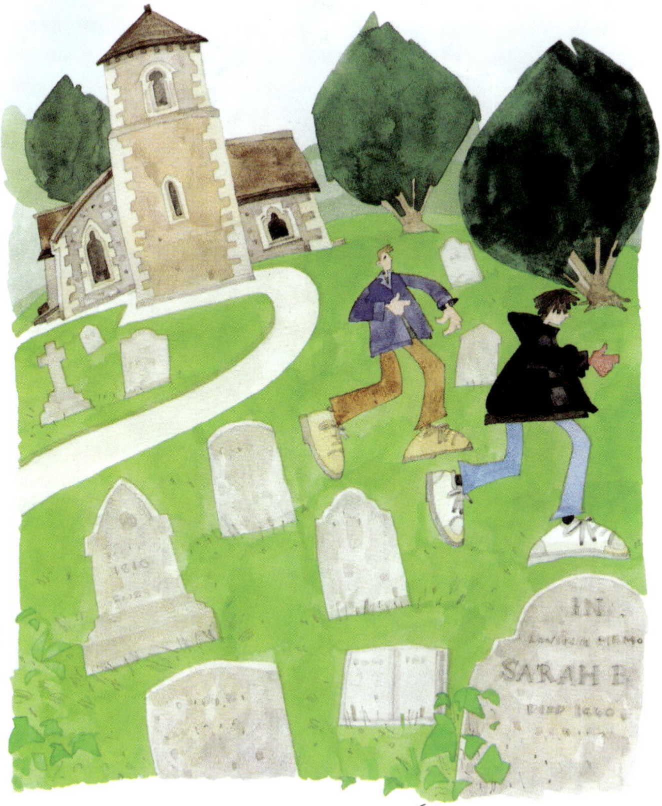

'There's a big drop on the other side,' he said. 'I'll go over first and you lower the bike down to me.' He dropped out of sight and Andrew, looking over the wall, saw him land, eight feet below, knee-deep in what looked like pea-plants. He lifted Victor's bicycle and heaved it over the wall. When Victor stretched up and took hold of it from beneath, Andrew followed it. The drop looked much more than eight feet while he was hanging by his hands from the top of the wall, and he felt like going back until he noticed that although his head was eight feet above the ground his shoes were five feet lower, so he let go and dropped, landing beside Victor.

'They are peas,' he said, as he picked himself up. 'Aren't they funny? I've never seen them so small. I thought they always grew up sticks.'

'Those go for freezing,' said Victor, wheeling the bicycle away under the shadow of the wall. They were walking on a little, greasy mud path and the pea-plants trailed across it. The pods went off like detonators under their shoes. 'They aren't picked by hand. They have to be small for the machine to pick them.'

When they came to the end of the wall, Victor struck out across the pea field, and there was a perfect salvo of exploding pods.

'Shouldn't we stay on the path?' said Andrew, looking round, warily.

'This is the path,' said Victor. 'That have to be ploughed in, every year and they set the crop over it. We can still use that. I think I'm the only person who do use it, that's why that don't show up.'

At that moment there was a terrific explosion, just behind them.

'We're being shot at,' cried Andrew, convinced that they were trespassing after all. He looked round for the gunman.

'That's the old bird-scarer,' said Victor, pointing to a machine that squatted among the pea plants a few yards away.

'It looks like a little cannon,' said Andrew, still twitching.

'Well, that is, really,' said Victor. 'That work off bottled gas. There's another one, down there. Don't worry, that won't go off again for a bit. Haven't you heard them before?'

'Yes, but I thought it was a gun. There's a man goes past our house, every night. He's got a gun.'

'That'll be my Dad, out after the pigeons,' said Victor. 'We have them for supper.'

'You eat pigeons?' said Andrew. Pigeons were pets: it was almost as bad as eating guinea-pigs.

'This is the loke,' said Victor as they came out of the pea field and through a gap in the hedge. 'That's our house, half way down. I'd ask you in but my Mum like to know if we've got anybody coming.' He turned in at the gate. I'll probably see you on Monday,' he said, as he scooted up the path. Andrew saw a cross face looking out of the window and hurried on, round the corner, into his own lane.

Toward Tiler's Cottage he overtook Mum, pushing Edward in the pram. Edward, with a gentle smile on his face, was strangling a banana.

'Where did you spring from?' said Mum. 'I thought you'd be home already.'

'I walked home with a friend,' said Andrew. 'He lives down the loke.'

'What's a loke?' said Mum, pleased that he had a friend, but not saying so.

'Half a lane,' said Andrew.

The Ghost of Grania O'Malley

Michael Morpurgo

Chapter Two: The Big Hill

Jessie Parsons and her family live on Clare Island. In this extract, Jessie tries to climb the Big Hill, which long ago had been the territory of Grania O'Malley, the Pirate Queen.

There had to be a mist or Jessie would not even try it. If she failed, and so far she had always failed, she wanted no one else to know of it, especially her mother and father. She'd lost count of how many times she'd lied to them about the Big Hill, about how she had made it all the way to the top. They mustn't see her. No one must see her. If she was going to fail again, then she would fail alone and unseen.

Old Mister Barney might see her, and probably often did, as she passed his shack at the bottom of the Big Hill, but he'd be the only one; and besides, he wouldn't tell anyone. Mister Barney kept himself to himself and minded his own business. He hardly ever spoke to a soul. Jessie was ten and he had spoken to her maybe half a dozen times in her entire life. He would wave at her through the window sometimes, but she was as sure as she could be that he would never spy on her. He just wasn't like that. There was smoke coming from his chimney and one of the chickens stood one-legged in the porch; but today, as Jessie walked across the clearing outside his shack, there was no sign of Mister Barney.

The mist cut the hill off halfway up and dwarfed it, but Jessie knew what was waiting for her up there, how high it really was, how hard it was going to be, and was daunted by it all over again.

Mole, her mother's black donkey, nudged her from behind. Mole would go with her. He went everywhere with her. More than once it had been Mole who had spoilt it, nudging her off balance at just the wrong moment.

There was a lot that annoyed her about her 'lousy palsy', as she often called it. But it was balance that was the real problem. Once she'd fallen over, it took so much of her energy to get up again that there was little left for the Big Hill itself. If she could just keep her rhythm going - one and two, one and two, one and two - if she could just keep on lurching, and not fall over, she knew that one day, some day, she'd have strength enough to reach the top of the Big Hill, and then she'd never have to lie about it again.

Mole rubbed his nose up against her back. 'All right, Mole,' said Jessie, clutching the donkey's neck to steady herself. 'I'm going, I'm going. It's all very well for you. You've got four good legs. I've only got two, and they won't exactly do what I tell them, will they?' She looked up at the Big Hill and took a deep breath. 'I'm telling you, Mole, today's the day. I can feel it inside me.' The donkey glanced at her and snorted. Jessie laughed. 'Race you to the top, big ears.'

She started well enough, leaning forward into the hill, willing her fumbling feet forward. She knew every rut and tussock of the track ahead - she'd sat down hard enough on most of them. Mole walked alongside her, browsing in the bracken. After a while he trotted on ahead, all tippy-toed, and disappeared into the mist. 'Clever clogs!' Jessie called after him, but then she tried all she could to put him out of her mind. She knew she had to concentrate. The path was wet from the mist, and slippery. One false step and she'd be on her bottom and that would be that - again.

She could hear Mole snorting somewhere up ahead. As like as not, he'd be at the waterfall by now. Jessie had reached the waterfall just once, the week before - it was as high as she'd ever gone on her own. That time, too, her legs had let her down. They wouldn't manage the stones and she'd tripped and fallen. She'd tried crawling, but she wasn't any better at crawling than she was at walking. She'd crawled on through the water, become too cold and had had to give up. Today would be different. Today she would not let herself give up. Today she would reach the top, no matter what. Today she would prove to Mrs Burke, to Marion Murphy, and to everyone else at school that she could climb the Big Hill just like they could.

She could see Mole up ahead of her now, drinking in the pool below the waterfall. Jessie's legs ached. She wanted so much to stop, but she knew that she mustn't, that rhythm was everything. She passed Mole and laughed out loud at him. 'Haven't you read the one about the hare and the tortoise?' she cried. 'See you at the top.' This was the spot where she'd come to grief the week before, the part of the track she most dreaded. The track rose steeply beside the waterfall, curling away out of sight and around the back of the hill. Every stone was loose here and until she reached the waterfall, *if* she reached the waterfall, the track would be more like a stream, the stones under her feet more like stepping stones. From now on she would have to be careful, very careful.

She was standing now on the very rock where she'd tripped last time. She punched the air with triumph and staggered on, on and up. She was in unknown territory now. Only on her father's back had she ever gone beyond this point and that was a long time ago when she was small. She felt her legs weakening all the while. She fought them, forcing them on. She breathed in deep, drawing what strength she could from the air, and that was when the mist filled her lungs. She coughed and had to go on coughing. Still she tried to go on.

She felt herself falling and knew she could do nothing about it. She threw her arm out to save herself and was relieved to see she was falling into the water. She would be wet, but at least she wasn't going to hurt herself. But she hadn't accounted for the stone just beneath the surface of the water. She never even felt the cold of the stream as it covered her face. There was an explosion of pain inside her head and a ringing in her ears that seemed as if it would never end. Then the world darkened suddenly around her. She tried to see through it, but she couldn't. She tried to breathe, but she couldn't.

She was dreaming of her father's 'creature' sculptures. They were all in the cottage and Smiley was telling them a story and they were laughing, cackling like witches. She woke suddenly. She was sitting propped up, her back against a boulder. Mole was grazing some way off, his tail whisking. Jessie's head throbbed and she put her hand to it. There was a lump under her

fingers, and it was sticky with blood. There was more blood in her ear and on her cheek too. She was soaked to the skin.
She wondered for some moments where she was and how she had got there. She remembered the climb up the Big Hill, and how she had fallen; and she realised then that she had failed yet again. Tears filled her eyes and she cried out loud, her fists clenched, her eyes closed to stop her tears.

She tasted the salt of her tears and brushed them away angrily.

'I'll get there, Mrs Burke,' she shouted. 'I'll get there, you'll see.'

From nowhere came a voice, a woman's voice, but almost low enough to be a man's. 'Course you will Jessie,' it said. 'But not if you sit there feeling all sorry for yourself.' Jessie looked around her. There was no one there. Mole glanced at her quizzically. He had stopped chomping. For one silly moment, Jessie imagined it might have been Mole talking, but then the voice went on. 'So you've a bit of a knock on your head. Are you going to let that stop you?' Mole was browsing again, tearing at the grass. So it couldn't be him talking. 'I'm not the donkey, Jessie. And I'll tell you something else for nothing, there's no point at all in your looking for me. I'm just a voice, that's all. Don't go worrying about it.'

'Who are you?' Jessie whispered, sitting up and wiping her nose with the back of her hand.

'Is that what they teach children these days? Can you not use a handkerchief like a proper person? Have you not got a handkerchief?'

'Yes,' said Jessie, still looking all around her, but frantically now.

'Then use it, why don't you?' Jessie searched out her handkerchief and blew her nose. 'That's better now,' the voice went on. 'I've always thought that you can tell a lot about folk from the way they treat their noses. There's pickers, there's wipers – like you – there's snifflers and, worst of all, there's trumpeters. You'll not believe this, but I once knew a queen, a real queen, I'm telling you - and she was a trumpeter. Worse still, she'd blow her nose on a handkerchief and she wouldn't throw it away like you or me. She'd use it again, honest she would. She'd use the same handkercief twice. Can you believe such a thing? And herself a queen! I told her straight out. I said: "There's no surer way to catch a cold and die than to use the same handkerchief twice." She was no one's fool, that queen. Oh no, she listened to me. She must have, because she lived on into a ripe old age, just like me. She died sitting up. Did you know that?'

Chuckling now, the voice seemed to be coming closer all the time. 'That queen, she wouldn't lie down for anyone, not even death. A lady after my own heart she was. English, mind, but she couldn't help that now, could she? Listen, Jessie, are you just going to sit there or are you going to get up on your feet and climb the Big Hill, like you said you would?'

'Who are you?' Jessie asked again. She was hoping against hope that maybe she was still asleep and dreaming it all. But she *was* bleeding and there *was* real blood on her fingers, on her head. So the voice had to be real too - unless she was going mad. That thought, that she might be going mad, frightened Jessie above everything else.

'It doesn't matter who I am,' said the voice, and it came from right beside her now, 'except that this is my hill you're walking on. I've been watching you these last weeks, we all have, the boys and me. They didn't think you'd make it, but I did. I was sure of it, so sure of it that I've a wager on it - five gold doubloons. And, Jessie, if there's one thing I hate losing, it's money. And here you are, sitting there like a pudding, crying your eyes out and wiping your nose with the back of your hand. I'm ashamed of you, Jessie.'

'I'm sorry,' said Jessie. 'I didn't mean to … '

'So you should be. I tell you what.' The voice was whispering in her ear. 'I'll make it worth your while. I'll leave a little something for you at the top of the hill. But if you want my little something, then you'll have to go up there and fetch it for yourself. How about it?'

Jessie was still thinking about what she should do when she felt strong arms under her shoulders, lifting her on to her feet and then holding her for a moment until she had steadied herself on her legs.

Then someone tapped her bottom. 'On your way, girl.' And Jessie found herself walking on, almost without meaning to, as if her legs where being worked by someone else. She looked behind her again and again to see if anyone was there. There was no one, only Mole ambling along, head lowered, ears back.

'Did you hear her?' Jessie whispered, as Mole came alongside. 'She's watching us, I know she is. Come on Mole, we've *got* to get to the top, we've got to.' And she lurched on up the Big Hill, rejoining the track beyond the waterfall.

The grass under her feet was spongy here; easier walking, easier falling too, she thought. She remembered how her father had galloped her on his back along this same grassy path, and how they'd fallen over and rolled down the hill together and into the bracken. She remembered too the rock-strewn gully ahead, and wondered how she was ever going to get past it. She went down on her hands and knees. It would be painful and slow, but it was the only way. There were brambles across the path that had to be pulled away, endless lacerating rocks to be negotiated. Jessie kept crawling until her wrists couldn't take it any more and she had to crawl on her elbows. That was when her knee slipped and her fingers wouldn't grasp and she slid backwards. She ended up in an ungainly heap, wedged against the rocks, knees and elbows barked and bleeding, and a vicious thorn stuck in the palm of her hand. She drew it out with her teeth and spat it on to the ground.

Mole was braying at her from somewhere further up the hill. Jessie looked up, shielding her eyes against the white of the sun that was breaking now through the mist. Mole was standing right on top of the Big Hill. He wasn't just calling her, he was taunting her. Jessie levered herself laboriously to her feet and swayed there for a moment, her head spinning. She closed her eyes, and then it all came flooding back.

April, the start of the summer term at school and they'd all of them gone, even the infants, up the Big Hill on a nature walk with Mrs Burke, her head teacher and the other bane of her life besides Marion Murphy. And Jessie had been the only one to be left behind with Miss Jefferson, the infant teacher. Miss Jefferson had insisted on holding her hand all the way to the beach, just in case, she said. They were going to find lots of interesting shells, she said, to make a shell picture. It was always shells or wild flowers with Miss Jefferson – she had her own wild flower meadow behind the school. But today it was shells.

Miss Jefferson foraged through the bladderwrack and the sea lettuce, whooping with joy every few seconds and talking nineteen to the dozen like she always did. It wasn't that Jessie didn't like her; she did. But she was forever fussing her, endlessly anxious that Jessie might fall, might be too cold, might be too tired. Jessie was used to that, used to her. It was being left behind that she really resented.

Despite all Miss Jefferson's enthusiastic encouragement she could not bring herself to care a fig about the shell picture. She wanted to be up there with them, with the others. All the while she kept her eye on the Big Hill. She could see them, a trail of children up near the summit now, Mrs Burke striding on ahead. She heard the distant cheer when they reached the top and she had to look away. Miss Jefferson understood and put her arm round her, but it was no comfort.

She had begged to be allowed to go up the Big Hill with the others, but Mrs Burke wouldn't hear of it. 'You'd slow us down, Jessie,' she'd said. 'And besides, you know you'd never reach the top.' And then she'd laughed. 'And I'm afraid you're far too big to carry.' That was the moment Jessie had decided she would climb the Big Hill, cerebral lousy palsy or not. Somehow or other she would do it, she'd drag herself up there if necessary.

She opened her eyes. Here she was, after two months of trying, within a stone's throw of the summit. This time there'd be no stopping her. 'Here I come!' she cried. 'Here I come!' And she launched herself up the hill. Several times her legs refused to do what she told them and threatened to buckle beneath her. Time and again, she felt herself reeling. She longed just to sit down and rest; but again and again she heard the voice in her head. 'You can do it, girl, you can do it.'

Where the words came from, or who spoke them, she neither knew nor cared any more. Nothing mattered but getting to the top. She was almost there when her legs simply folded on her, and she found herself on her knees. She crawled the last metre or so over mounds of soft thrift and then collapsed. Mole came over to her and nuzzled her neck with his warm whiskery nose. She clung to Mole's mane and hauled herself up on to her feet.

There below her lay the whole of Clare Island, and all around the grey-green sea, with the island of Inishturk far to the south. And when she turned her face into the wind, there was the mainland and the islands of Clew Bay floating in the sea like distant dumplings. She was on top of the world. She lifted her hands to the sky and laughed out loud and into the wind, the tears running down her face. Mole looked on, each of his ears turning independently. Jessie's legs collapsed and she sat down with a sudden jolt that knocked the breath out of her for a moment, and stunned her into sanity.

Only then did she begin to reflect on all that had happened to her on the Big Hill that morning. There could be no doubt that she had made it to the top, unless of course she was still in the middle of some wonderful dream. But the more she thought about it, the more she began to doubt her memory of the climb, the fall in the stream, the disembodied voice that had spoken to her, the arms that had helped her to her feet, the words in her head that had urged her on to the top. It could all have been some extraordinary hallucination. That would make sense of it. But then, what about the bump on her head? And there was something else she couldn't understand. Someone must have rescued her from the stream. But who? Maybe it was all the bump on the head, maybe that was why she was hearing voices. And maybe that was why her memory was deceiving her. She had to be sure, really sure. She had to test it.

'Hello?' she ventured softly. 'Are you still there? I did it, didn't I? I won your bet for you. Are you there?' There was no one, nothing, except a solitary humming bumble-bee, a pair of gulls wheeling overhead and Mole munching nearby. Jessie went on, 'Are you anyone? Are you someone? Are you just a bump on the head or what? Are you real? Say something, please.' But no one said anything. Something rustled behind her. Jessie swung round and saw a rabbit scuttling away into the bracken, white trail bobbing. She noticed there were rabbit droppings all over the summit. She flicked at one of them and it bounced off the side of a rock, a giant granite rock shaped by the wind and weather into a perfect bowl, and in the bowl was a pool of shining water fed by a spring from above it.

Jessie hadn't been thirsty until now. She crawled over, grasped the lip of the rock and hauled herself up. She put her mouth into the water like Mole did and drank deep. Water had never been so welcome to her as it was that morning on the summit of the Big Hill. She was wiping her mouth when she saw something glinting at the bottom of the pool. It looked like a large ring, brass maybe, like one of the curtain rings they had at home in the sitting room. She reached down into the water and picked it out.

'I am a woman of my word.' The same voice, from behind her somewhere. 'Didn't I say I'd leave a little something for you?' In her exhaustion, in her triumph, Jessie had quite forgotten all about the promised 'little something'. She backed herself up against the rock. 'Don't be alarmed, Jessie, I'll not hurt you. I've never hurt a single soul that didn't deserve it. You did a fine thing today, Jessie, a fine thing; and what's better still, you won me my wager. I'm five gold doubloons richer, not that I've a lot to spend it on, mind. None of us have, but that's by the by. None of the boys thought you could do it, but I did. And I like to be right. It's a family failing of ours. "Her mother's an O'Malley," I told them. "So Jessie's half an O'Malley. She'll do it, just watch." And we did watch you and you did do it. The earring's yours, girl. To be honest with you I've not a lot of use for such things these days. Look after it, won't you?'

The Hobbit

J.R.R. TOLKIEN

Chapter Four: Over Hill and Under Hill

Bilbo Baggins is a comfort-loving, unambitious hobbit who is a reluctant partner on a quest for dragon-guarded gold. Thorin Oakenshield leads the quest. In this extract, Bilbo, Thorin and their friends encounter a group of very angry goblins.

'Thorin the dwarf at your service!' he replied – it was merely a polite nothing. 'Of the things which you suspect and imagine we had no idea at all. We sheltered from a storm in what seemed a convenient cave and unused; nothing was further from our thoughts than inconveniencing goblins in any way whatever.' That was true enough!

'Um!' said the Great Goblin. 'So you say! Might I ask what you were doing in the mountains at all, and where you were coming from, and where you were going to? In fact I should like to know all about you. Not that it will do you much good, Thorin Oakenshield, I know too much about your folk already; but let's have the truth, or I will prepare something particularly uncomfortable for you!'

'We were on a journey to visit our relatives, our nephews and nieces, and first, second, and third cousins, and the other descendants of our grandfathers, who live on the East side of these truly hospitable mountains,' said Thorin, not quite knowing what to say all at once in a moment, when obviously the exact truth would not do at all.

'He is a liar, O truly tremendous one!' said one of the drivers. 'Several of our people were struck by lightning in the cave, when we invited these creatures to come below; and they are as dead as stones. Also he has not explained this!' He held out the sword which Thorin had worn, the sword which came from the Trolls' lair.

The Great Goblin gave a truly awful howl of rage when he looked at it, and all his soldiers gnashed their teeth, clashed their shields, and stamped. They knew the sword at once. It had killed hundreds of goblins in its time, when the fair elves of Gondolin hunted them in the hills or did battle before their walls. They had called it Orcrist, Goblin-cleaver, but the goblins called it simply Biter. They hated it and hated worse any one that carried it.

'Murderers and elf-friends!' the Great Goblin shouted. 'Slash them! Beat them! Bite them! Gnash them! Take them away to dark holes full of snakes, and never let them see the light again!' He was in such a rage that he jumped off his seat and himself rushed at Thorin with his mouth open.

Just at that moment all the lights in the cavern went out, and the great fire went off poof! into a tower of blue glowing smoke, right up to the roof, that scattered piercing white sparks all among the goblins.

The yells and yammering, croaking, jibbering and jabbering; howls, growls and curses; shrieking and skriking, that followed were beyond description. Several hundred wild cats and wolves being roasted slowly alive together would not have compared with it. The sparks were burning holes in the goblins, and the smoke that now fell from the roof made the air thick for even their eyes to see through. Soon they were falling over one another and rolling in

heaps on the floor, biting and kicking and fighting as if they had all gone mad.

Suddenly a sword flashed in its own light. Bilbo saw it go right through the Great Goblin as he stood dumbfounded in the middle of his rage. He fell dead, and the goblin soldiers fled before the sword shrieking into the darkness.

The sword went back into its sheath. 'Follow me quick!' said a voice fierce and quiet; and before Bilbo understood what had happened he was trotting along again, as fast as he could trot, at the end of the line, down more dark passages with the yells of the goblin-hall growing fainter behind him. A pale light was leading them on.

'Quicker, quicker!' said the voice. 'The torches will soon be relit.'

'Half a minute!' said Dori who was at the back next to Bilbo, and a decent fellow. He made the hobbit scramble on his shoulders as best he could with his tied hands, and then off they all went at a run, with a clink-clink of chains, and many a stumble, since they had no hands to steady themselves with. Not for a long while did they stop, and by that time they must have been right down in the very mountain's heart.

Then Gandalf lit up his wand. Of course it was Gandalf; but just then they were too busy to ask how he got there. He took out his sword again, and again it flashed in the dark by itself. It burned

with a rage that made it gleam if goblins were about; now it was bright as blue flame for delight in the killing of the great lord of the cave. It made no trouble whatever of cutting through the goblin-chains and setting all the prisoners free as quickly as possible. This sword's name was Glamdring the Foe-hammer if you remember. The goblins just called it Beater, and hated it worse than Biter if possible. Orcrist, too, had been saved; for Gandalf had brought it along as well, snatching it from one of the terrified guards. Gandalf thought of most things; and though he could not do everything, he could do a great deal for friends in a tight corner.

'Are we all here?' said he, handing his sword back to Thorin with a bow. 'Let me see: one – that's Thorin; two, three, four, five, six, seven, eight, nine, ten, eleven; where are Fili and Kili? Here they are! Twelve, thirteen – and here's Mr Baggins: fourteen! Well, well! it might be worse, and then again it might be a good deal better. No ponies, and no food, and no knowing quite where we are, and hordes of angry goblins just behind! On we go!'

On they went. Gandalf was quite right: they began to hear goblin noises and horrible cries far behind in the passages they had come through. That sent them on faster than ever, and as poor Bilbo could not possibly go half as fast – for dwarves can roll along at a tremendous pace, I can tell you, when they have to – they took it in turn to carry him on their backs.

Still goblins go faster than dwarves, and these goblins knew the way better (they had made the paths themselves), and were madly angry; so that do what they could the dwarves heard the cries and howls getting closer and closer. Soon they could hear even the flap of the goblin feet, many many feet which seemed only just round the last corner. The blink of red torches could be seen behind them in the tunnel they were following; and they were getting deadly tired.

'Why, O why did I ever leave my hobbit-hole!' said poor Mr Baggins bumping up and down on Bombur's back.

'Why, O why did I ever bring a wretched little hobbit on a treasure hunt!' said poor Bombur, who was fat, and staggered along with the sweat dripping down his nose in his heat and terror.

At this point Gandalf fell behind, and Thorin with him. They turned a sharp corner. 'About turn!' he shouted. 'Draw your sword Thorin!'

There was nothing else to be done; and the goblins did not like it. They came scurrying round the corner in full cry, and found Goblin-cleaver, and Foe-hammer shining cold and bright right in their astonished eyes. The ones in front dropped their torches and gave one yell before they were killed. The ones behind yelled still more, and leaped back knocking over those that were running after them. 'Biter and Beater!' they shrieked; and soon they were all in confusion, and most of them were hustling back the way they had come.

It was quite a long while before any of them dared to turn that corner. By that time the dwarves had gone on again, a long, long, way on into the dark tunnels of the goblins' realm. When the goblins discovered that, they put out their torches and they slipped on soft shoes, and they chose out their very quickest runners with the sharpest eyes and ears. These ran forward, as swift as weasels in the dark, and with hardly any more noise than bats.

That is why neither Bilbo, nor the dwarves, nor even Gandalf heard them coming. Nor did they see them. But they were seen by the goblins that ran silently up behind, for Gandalf was letting his wand give out a faint light to help the dwarves as they went along.

Quite suddenly Dori, now at the back again carrying Bilbo, was grabbed from behind in the dark. He shouted and fell; and the hobbit rolled off his shoulders into the blackness, bumped his head on hard rock, and remembered nothing more.

The Deerstone

MAEVE FRIEL

Chapter Two: Luke

Paud has been sent to summer camp by his parents who have gone on holiday abroad. He is lonely and unhappy. When he goes on a trip to Glendalough, he is catapulted back in time and meets a boy of his own age who's as lonely as he is …

The lake was long and narrow, surrounded on three sides by steep thickly wooded mountains. It was absolutely still, shimmering in the cold hard sunshine. For a few moments Paud was taken aback and stared open-mouthed at its serene beauty – but not for long! It seemed too good an opportunity to miss – with no one in sight he could easily have a quick swim.

'It's deep and intensely cold and far too dangerous,' the group leader, Miss Kelly, had said that morning when she was making all her boring announcements on the coach. 'Lakes are very unpredictable places so swimming is absolutely forbidden at all times. Don't even think about it!'

But she would never know, thought Paud.

He pulled off his sneakers and socks, then his shirt and jeans and made a neat pile which he weighed down with the plastic bag which contained his lunch. Helen made a mean lunch, it had to be said, ham sandwiches, a banana, crisps, a carton of orange juice and a couple of small Mars bars. After the swim, he'd have the crisps.

He dipped a toe in the water. That woman was right – it was freezing – but it was too late to chicken out now. He flung his boxers in the direction of the rest of his things and made a long expert dive into the ice-cold water. It folded over him, a strong undertow pulling, dragging him down to the murky floor of the lake.

Paud fought against it, struggling to rise again to the surface, spluttering and petrified with the cold. His breath came in short shallow gasps, real panic overtaking him. It was as if some evil force existed in the lake, some trapped beast sucking him down into its watery lair. With a massive effort of will, he struck out in a strong crawl for the shore again, furious at himself for being so stupid. He should never have come here alone – what if he had got cramps and drowned? No one would ever find him.

As he neared the shore, he stopped to tread water – where were his clothes? Surely he had not swum so far from where he left them. Everything seemed alien now, unfamiliar. Blinded by tears of rage and shivering with cold, Paud scrambled up on to the rocks to get his bearings.

Behind him, a low voice said, 'Who are you? Where have you come from?'

Paud swung around in alarm. A boy, about the same age as himself, twelve maybe, was sitting a few yards away. He was dressed in a long brown tunic made of rough-looking wool and his blond hair was cut in an unkind round bowl-shape like that of some of the wallies at school.

'Monkstown,' Paud answered too quickly. He didn't like being caught off-guard like that – and with no clothes on!

'Are you an apprentice? Is Monks' Town like Glendalough?'

Paud looked at the other boy. This is some weirdo, he was thinking, a culchie for sure.

'No, Monkstown is not like Glendalough – it's part of the city, that's Dublin city of course,' he added in a sarcastic voice, in case this weirdo thought he was talking about Cork or somewhere.

'How far is it from here? Do you mean the new abbey in Baltinglass?'

'Look, it has nothing to do with monks. It's about an hour from here, if you must know, probably less if you come by car and not in a stupid bus.'

'What is a bus? Is it a type of horse?'

'Are you having me on, or what? I'm off.' Paud turned away, spotting his clothes now, less than twenty metres away, but the strange boy followed him at a run.

'What an odd sack you have,' he said as Paud picked up the plastic carrier bag. 'What is the writing on it?'

‘I think you need your head examined. It says whatever it always says on a Superquinn bag. Go away!’

But the boy still stood, staring at him as Paud pulled on his shorts.

‘Does Brother Brendan know you are here? Have you come with news for Abbot Laurence?’

‘Brother who? Look, are you here with some sort of fancy dress party? What’s with the outfit?’ Paud pointed at the boy’s brown tunic. He was feeling better now that he had some clothes on himself.

‘I do not understand,’ replied the boy. ‘I am Lugaid, son of Dermot, but here they call me Luke. I am Brother Brendan’s pupil. He is teaching me to write.’

‘Are you at some kind of special school then? Why are you not on holiday? Don’t tell me that is the school uniform.’ Paud laughed.

Luke pointed to the far shore of the lake. ‘My father has left me here in the care of the monks. Brother Brendan is down there, walking with Fidelmus. They are gathering yarrow to make infusions.’

Paud slowly pulled on his jeans and stood up to close the zip. Something about the boy was beginning to make him feel uneasy.

‘Do you live with monks all the time? Don’t you go home at all?’

‘This is my home now, since my father remarried. He lives at Ferns now with his new wife, Mor. She is the step-sister of Laurence, the abbot here, so my father left me with him. Now Laurence is to go to the new cathedral in Dublin so Brendan is my tutor.' Luke stopped and bit his lip. 'My father will send for me, I'm sure, when I am older and can help him, but now is a bad time for him. He has many enemies. But Dublin is his now.' He rubbed a grimy fist under his eyes.

Embarrassed, Paud flopped down onto the ground and began to rummage about in his lunch bag for crisps. He hated people crying – there was always somebody crying in the dormitory at school – though this guy seemed to have more than enough cause. Imagine being abandoned like that by his father to live with monks all the time!

'Here, have a bag of crisps. They're salt and vinegar, okay?' He threw the crisps onto Luke's lap. 'Go on, open them.' Luke picked up the packet of crisps gingerly and examined it, slowly turning it over and over in his hands.

'Are you an Ostman, a foreigner?' he asked finally, watching Paud carefully from beneath his fringe as Paud pulled on his socks and began to lace up his trainers.

Paud stopped. The boy was picking bits of grass from between his toes and had left the crisps untouched on the shingle beside him.

Something strange is going on here, thought Paud, looking around him. Everything looks different. There shouldn't be so many trees and I don't remember seeing those stone beehive things. He started to run back in the direction of the lower lake, staring around him in disbelief as the awful truth began to dawn on him.

'Miss Kelly,' he screamed, 'where are you? I'm lost.' His voice came back at him, ricocheting off the sides of the mountains.

'Tell me who you are. I will help you find the person you were shouting for.' The strange boy had been running behind him all the time and had caught up with him.

The two boys stared at one another, their eyes meeting for the first time. Both gave a start of recognition as each saw his own face in the other. Apart from their haircuts, they were the image of one another, as like as identical twins.

'What year is this?' asked Paud.

'It is the year of Our Lord eleven hundred and sixty two.'

'No, no, it isn't,' said Paud despairingly, his eyes wide with alarm. 'It's 1991.' He grabbed Luke by the shoulders. 'It's 1991, believe me. I must get out of here. Help me.'

Paud's face had become completely drained of colour. Pale-faced and looking younger than his twelve years, he clung to Luke as the tears streamed down his face.

'How, how can this have happened?' he sobbed.

'Why has it happened?' countered Luke. 'God must have sent you here to do something.'

'Don't be silly. God has nothing to do with it. I've travelled through time. There must be a logical explanation.' Paud had seen programmes on television about time travel; it was probably commoner than people thought. All he had to do was to get back in the loop or whatever had caused it and he would be back in his own time again. Oh God, the awfulness of it all. Would he ever escape?

'Well,' said Luke doubtfully, 'the best thing is to hide somewhere until we know what to do. Fidelmus and Brendan will be coming back this way any time now and they should not see you. They might think you were a spy or a runaway and lock you up.' He solemnly handed Paud the carrier bag and the bag of crisps which he had picked up at the lakeside when Paud had run off. 'Follow me.'

He took off like a hunting dog after a rabbit, up above the shore of the lake, hopping from stone to stone, skilfully avoiding the clumps of heather and high nettles which pricked and stung Paud's arms. They began to climb through the trees on the southern side of the lake, pushing their way clear through the dense undergrowth of holly, ivy and bramble. Startled rabbits bolted from their burrows as the two boys raced past. A wood pigeon crashed noisily from its tree perch, crying alarm. Here and there they had to jump across narrow rivulets of water which splashed down the valley into the lake below. Eventually Luke stopped. They had reached a clearing on a high promontory overlooking the lake. On it stood a solitary monk's cell in the shape of a stone beehive.

'No one comes here any more. They call it St Kevin's cell – he lived here hundreds of years ago and started the monastery here in Glendalough. We all live down there by the other lake. Can you see where the round tower is?' Luke pointed far in the distance where they could just make out the buildings of the monastic city dominated by the tall round tower where Paud had sneaked away from his summer school group. 'There is one church near here,

St Reefert's, but nobody goes there until the evening. The abbot likes to make evening devotions there for that is the burial place of his family, the royal clan of the O'Tooles.'

'My head hurts,' said Paud, throwing himself on the ground next to the beehive. 'I'm sorry if I was rude to you before. Sit down beside me and help me figure this out.'

'I've been thinking,' he said after a few minutes. 'I must have changed some time before I went for the swim. I had been sitting on a stone beside the stream just beyond the turnstile in the stone wall and I made a wish. I said something like, I wish someone needed me. I wish something different would happen. I was feeling really bad at the time because my parents have sent me away too, just like yours. Well, not exactly like yours, but they have gone away and left me behind and I hardly ever see them any more.'

Luke nodded. 'Where were you exactly when you made the wish?'

'At a pile of rocks beside the river. One of the stones is like a bowl. It had water in it.'

'And the one beside it has marks, like fingers, on the side?'

'That's it, exactly!' shouted Paud. 'You know it too. I was sitting on the one with the fingermarks.'

Luke nodded again. 'We call that cairn the Deerstone. The old monks say it has magical powers but no one ever believed them. Malachi, the stonemason – he is the leader of the men who are building the new priory outside the city – told me the story about it, about how the hollow stone saved the lives of twin baby boys. But that happened in the time of St Kevin, ages ago.'

'Have you ever made a wish on the Deerstone?'

'Yes, I wished for my father's enemies to be defeated and for him to come and take me home. And I wished for a friend.'

'Did your wishes some true?'

'I don't know. I just made the wish this morning.'

The boys looked at one another, not knowing what to make of this.

'Come on, Luke, let's get back to the Deerstone and find out if it really has the power. If I make a wish, I probably can get back to my own time.' Paud leapt up and started to run down into the woods.

'Stop, wait, Paud, we can't go there now.'

Paud stopped running and wheeled around angrily. 'Why not?' he demanded.

'It's always crowded around there – if you go anywhere near there dressed like that, you will be seized. They will think you are a foreigner, a spy, maybe the Devil!'

'What do you suggest that I do?'

'I think we'll have to stay hidden until dark. The lay-brothers and the monks spend the day coming and going to the mill and tending the cattle and the pigs down by the lower lake until then.
At midday everyone gathers for prayers and that means many people crossing the river near the stones. You see, the abbot is building a new priory down in the woods on the opposite side of the river to the rest of the city and there are many stonemasons and craftsmen working there now. There are more people in Glendalough than ever before.'

'But I can't stay hidden all day long. I'll have to chance it.' Paud was desperate to get away, so desperate he couldn't even think about how or why such an extraordinary thing had happened to him. He just wanted everything back to normal as fast as possible.

Luke nodded gravely. 'I've got an idea. You wait here – I won't be long – hide in the cell if you see or hear people coming. I'll go and find you something … something less strange to wear.

Then you can just walk over to the Deerstone and make your wish.' He started to walk away, then added, 'Are you hungry? I don't know if I can find any food. I'm always hungry.'

Paul grinned. 'No problem – I have food, look. Look, Luke – I like the sound of that.' He opened his carrier bag and took out the banana and the foil-wrapped packet of sandwiches.

'What is that?' asked Luke, pointing to the banana. 'Is that food?' He smelled it doubtfully. 'It doesn't look like anything I know. How do you eat this?'

Paul peeled the banana and broke it in two. 'Here, try it. It's called a banana.'

Luke reached for the fruit and squeezed it between his thumb and forefinger.

'It tastes good. What else have you got?' He looked wistfully at the silver package.

'Go on then, open it.'

Luke raised the pack of sandwiches to his nose and gave it a good sniff.

'It smells like meat, I think, but I don't know how to eat it. Is this a skin too?' Paud took back the parcel and unwrapped the silver foil 'skin', enjoying the other boy's puzzlement. For a moment he had forgotten his awful predicament and was showing off his novelties like a conjurer on television taking surprises out of a top hat: 'See, this is just shiny paper. And this is bread, white bread although brown is better for you – and this is cooked ham.'

Luke took one of the sandwiches and examined it thoughtfully. 'It doesn't look like bread. Our bread is dark. I think I prefer the nabana.'

'Banana, you wally!' Paud punched him lightly on the chest.

'What is a wally, Paud?'

'You are a wally,' replied Paud, grabbing his new friend and wrestling him to the ground.

At that moment the silence of the valley was shattered by the bells of Glendalough's seven churches, hidden from sight but less than a mile distant, ringing out in loud urgent peals. Luke struggled free from Paud's grasp and jumped to his feet in alarm.

'What is it Luke? What does all the ringing mean?'

'It means danger, Paud. The city is under attack. It's a raid. Follow me!'

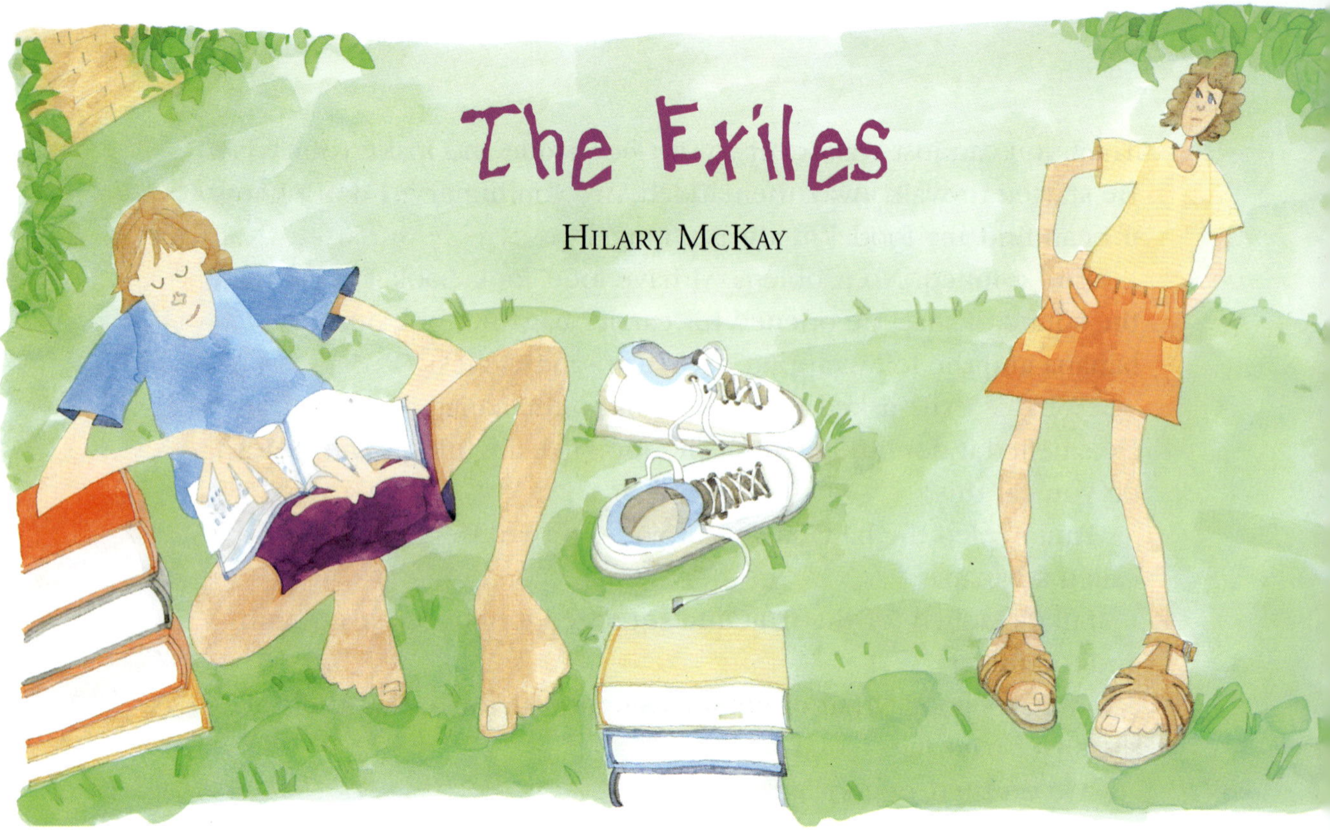

The Exiles

HILARY MCKAY

Chapter One

There was red brick in every direction. The back of the house and the fronts of the coal sheds enclosed two sides of the garden, and a high wall surrounded the rest, defending it from the neighbours in one direction, and the back alley (commonly knows as Gassy Pad), in the other.

It was the last weekend before the summer holidays.

Naomi Conroy crouched uncomfortably at the end of the garden reading a book. As usual, she had spent her Saturday morning at the town library, searching the too familiar shelves for something new. On her left was the stack of books she had read since she returned, and on her right was the pile she hadn't opened yet. She kept her elbow leaning on that pile to guard them from her permanently book-hungry sisters. Even now, she could feel herself being watched, and without looking up knew that Ruth was hovering close by, waiting for her to finish, when by law of the family the book would become common property, free for anyone to read.

Ruth watched the flickering of her sister's eyes as they moved across the page. She watched Naomi's grubby fingers curl and turn the pages over. She measured the thickness of book left to read, compared it to that read already, estimated the time it would take in minutes, deducted an amount for half pages and illustrations and sighed. Ruth was banned from the library. The librarian was holding her tickets to ransom in the hope of extracting at least part of the amount Ruth owed to the library in fines.

'But I'm one of your best customers,' Ruth had raged when this ultimatum was delivered.

'Worst customers,' corrected the librarian. And so Ruth (who had no money and would not have handed it over if she had) was reduced to surviving on the books her sisters chose and grudgingly handed over.

Naomi finished the chapter and closed the book. For a few seconds she could not see, and then her eyes refocused on the small, sunshiny garden. It was overcrowded, she thought. Too many plants, too many scattered belongings, too many book-starved sisters waiting to pounce.

Naomi was eleven years old, and Ruth was thirteen. They were the Big Ones. Phoebe and Rachel, aged six and eight, were the Little Ones. Although Ruth and Naomi had been known as the Big Ones since Rachel's arrival into the family, they still resented it. It gave them an uncomfortable feeling of being shoved on from behind, and neither of them took kindly to being shoved.

'One more week,' Ruth remarked, 'and then we'll be finished with school. That'll be one less torture anyway.'

'I'd rather be at school than stuck here all summer,' Naomi answered. 'I'd rather do anything. Even prison would be better.' She rolled over onto her back, pillowing her head on the pile of books. 'Solitary confinement, everyone locked out except me, that's what I'd like.'

'Anything for a change,' agreed Ruth while gently easing a book away from Naomi's heap. 'We ought to run away.'

'I know.'

'Like Robert did,' said Ruth, referring to an uncle who had made family history by disappearing in his youth and never coming back.

The book came away with a jerk and there was a short fight.

'Yes,' agreed Naomi, when it was over, 'but the trouble with running away is where to run to. If we went anywhere where we know someone we'd be sent back, and if we went anywhere where we don't, then we'd be lost. It's knowing where to start.'

'We'd start here,' said Ruth, sucking her bleeding knuckle.

'Well, then, it's knowing where to end.'

'Yes.'

The garden was quiet as they pondered, not for the first time, the problems of running away.

At the other end of what their father, Mr Conroy, liked to call The Lawn, Rachel and Phoebe were racing stolen maggots around the lid of a tin. The maggots belonged to Mr Conroy, and were bought for his fishing on Sundays. As well as the usual revolting white ones there were others, dyed, for some unfathomable reason, pink and green. Rachel always took a pink one, and Phoebe a green. They scooped them out of the tin with the silver spoon that belonged in the tea-caddy, appropriated for the purpose by Rachel. Maggot racing already showed signs of becoming the summer's main occupation. The rules were very strict. You could prod your maggot in the right direction, but not push him forwards. If they stopped you must allow them to start again of their own accord. Rachel always prodded hers with a blade of grass, but Phoebe usually favoured a matchstick. Maggots responded better to matchstick prodding, but it tended to wear them out faster. Phoebe's green maggot was beginning to look very limp.

'He's nearly dead,' said Rachel.

'He's just too hot,' replied Phoebe. 'Anyway, I'm fed up of this. I'm going to bury him now.' The career of a racing maggot inevitably ended in burial. It hid the evidence. What happened to the maggots afterwards was a mystery, although Rachel and Phoebe had often tried digging them up again to find out. Perhaps they crawled away, or a bird ate them. Either would be better than their original fate on the end of a hook.

'Did you put the lids back on the tins?' called Ruth from across the garden, remembering a time when this precaution had been forgotten, and the maggots had climbed the impossibly smooth sides of the tin, and escaped all over the tool shed.

'Did we?' asked Phoebe.

'Hope not,' said Naomi as Rachel hurried away to check, 'we could do with a bit of excitement.'

Phoebe finished patting the earth smooth over the maggots' graves and remarked, 'I wish something would happen.'

'Well, it won't,' said Ruth.

Ruth's gloomy conviction that It Wouldn't was based on the fact that, so far, It Never Had. Mrs Conroy, perhaps as a result of a rather too exciting childhood of her own, had carefully chosen to marry a man of such serene good nature that it was astonishing he survived at all. It was rather sad that two people whose only ambition was a life of security and peace should have been blessed with Ruth, Naomi, Rachel and Phoebe. Certainly they had done nothing to deserve it. Ruth, Naomi and Rachel had been welcomed to their quiet world with old-fashioned, gentle names, suitable to the natures their parents hoped they would develop. By the time that Phoebe was born, however, Mr and Mrs Conroy had become rather disillusioned. They did not give Phoebe a name that they hoped she would be like, they gave her the name they expected her to be like, for Ruth, Naomi and Rachel showed very few signs of old-fashioned gentleness. And as Phoebe grew up it became increasingly apparent that neither did she.

Mr and Mrs Conroy didn't own a car, wouldn't buy a television, disliked the thought of allowing pets into an already chaotic household, and could never quite afford to go on holidays. Naturally this made things somewhat difficult for their daughters, who, partly from personal inclination and partly in self-defence, maintained a carefully fostered defiance towards the world in general and school in particular.

'How awful to be you!' a girl in school had once remarked to Naomi, on hearing for the first time of her family's general differentness.

'Awful!' exclaimed Naomi, indignantly and untruthfully. 'What would be awful for people like you, boring people, isn't awful at all for people like me.'

'What sort of people are you supposed to be then?' demanded her questioner.

'I am Me,' said Naomi, 'and you are only you.'

Nobody was allowed to pity a Conroy girl. Depending on their latest rebellion they might be admired or feared or isolated, and such reactions were bearable, even desirable. Patronage was not. They went to frightful extremes to avoid it.

The summer weekend drifted on, exhausting itself and its participants with non-events. Sunday afternoon ended in Sunday Tea, varied and bountiful, and prepared, as always, by Mrs Conroy alone with no help from her daughters. The evening ran its usual course. Mrs Conroy dragged her husband from under his newspaper to spray the roses, her daughters from behind their library books to finish their homework, school uniforms from under beds to be exclaimed over in horror (but nothing else), and afterwards, having found occupations for everybody but herself, sat down and watched them work.

'I don't think this day will ever end,' she sighed.

Rachel and Phoebe were bathed, clean-pyjamad, and got rid of.

Naomi toiled through the dregs of her homework and was dismissed.

Ruth escaped.

Mr and Mrs Conroy, after weak tea and milk chocolate biscuits, locked the doors and withdrew.

Sunday night darkness seeped through the house.

All day long it had hung around waiting, hunched under the stairs, reeking in the shoe cupboard, shivering in the bottom of vases. Now it was loose.

Rachel and Phoebe slept in bunk beds packed with teddy bears, colouring books and stray lumps of Lego. Phoebe in the bottom bunk dreamed of crocodiles, the ones that lived in the front room behind the settee. There was nothing to be afraid of as long as you poked crisps into their mouths, and there were plenty of crisps left over from tea. Happily in her sleep Phoebe fed the dream crocodiles. Beneath the bedclothes her fingers moved, picking up crisps. Phoebe was safe in the dark; it never frightened her. Sometimes she woke herself up, singing loudly.

Rachel, in the top bunk because she was the eldest of the two, slept with her back jammed against the wall as far from the edge as possible. It was very uncomfortable. She had fallen asleep with her face resting on her hard brown plait, and it was printing a pattern of twists across her cheek. She did not dream, but all through her sleep hung a nervous distrust of the edge of her bed.

The dark was thickest and blackest in Ruth and Naomi's room, where huge old blue velvet curtains hung, smothering the windows. The curtains had faded round the hems to a browny-grey colour, and they held in Ruth and Naomi and the dark like gaolers.

Ruth lay awake, staring at nothing and thinking. One day, she dreamed, she would spend summer in the countryside, somewhere hilly, not like the Lincolnshire flatness she was accustomed to. She would have two houses – one for herself, and one for her family to come and visit her in – and she would be a famous … a famous … a famous what? Well, famous anyway, and very rich of course …

'Are you awake?' hissed Naomi through the dark.

'I'm thinking.'

'What about?'

'When I'm rich.'

'Huh!'

Silence for a while.

'Is that all you're thinking about?' asked Naomi eventually.

'One more week of school.'

'Yucky-pucky,' said Naomi, and fell asleep.

Mrs Conroy was dreaming of being lost in a strange town. She dreamt the same dream every night, but tonight she was rescued and returned to her safe dark bedroom by Mr Conroy, who seemed (from his kicking) to be dreaming of football.

19 Railway Street

MICHAEL SCOTT AND MORGAN LLYWELYN

Chapter Six

1776, orphaned but wealthy Sophie Rutledge lives a life of privilege in a fine Georgian house in Dublin. 1907, Mickser Lawless and his impoverished family occupy the same house now a tenement. Although one hundred and thirty years separate them, Sophie and Mickser are about to meet for the first time …

Sophie stood at the window and gazed down into the moonlit street below. 'I wish I were dead,' she said. But she did not mean it, she was merely trying on the words. She did not even know what dead meant, not really. Mama and Papa were dead, lying somewhere at the bottom of the sea. No matter how she tried she could not imagine them there, nor what it must be like for them.

Being dead.

In spite of the flannel dressing-gown she wore over her cambric nightdress, Sophie shuddered. Her bedchamber was cold. At sundown a chambermaid had come to light the fire, but the cheerful blaze had long since dwindled to a few glowing coals. They could not chase away the chill she felt inside. And she was hungry. Her stomach was growling in a way no lady's ever should.

Mademoiselle was always trying to make a lady of her. Perhaps the hated governess had been ordered to prepare her to be Robert's wife. What was it? Did he mean to marry her as soon as she was properly polished? Sometimes he looked at her in such a strange, speculative way …

The room seemed to be growing colder and the shadows in the corners were writhing into sinister shapes. Sophie had been unable to fall asleep in the big four-poster bed; she felt suffocated by its heavy draperies. What a cheerless place her bedchamber had become. Leaning on the windowsill, she addressed the friendly face of the moon. 'I would not marry Cousin Robert if he had a thousand pounds,' she said. 'Not even a *million* pounds!' She had no clear idea of how much a thousand pounds might be, never mind a million. She just liked the drama of the words.

Cold wind slammed against the glass, forcing her to take a step backward. But there was no place warm and safe to go. If only she were still in the nursery!

Then Sophie had an inspiration. She would reclaim some of the treasures Cousin Robert had taken from the nursery. Hidden in her bedchamber, they would keep her company on nights like this when her loneliness and unhappiness became unbearable. Dearly loved items from a childhood fast retreating into memory could be secreted at the back of the wardrobe, or even in the bedside cabinet with her chamber pot. Mademoiselle would never find them. She was only interested in what she considered valuables.

Once she had the idea Sophie could not wait to act upon it. She wrapped her dressing-gown more snugly around herself and went to the door. The handle turned silently. A moment later she stood on the second-storey landing.

With her head cocked to one side, she listened intently. The house was quiet. Only the wind was awake, stalking around the walls outside, rattling windows and seeking entry. But 19 Mecklenburg Street was solidly built, not even a cold draught could enter.

So why am I so cold? wondered the girl as she tiptoed down the curving front staircase. In a cloakroom off the entrance hall was a green baize door that opened into a service passage lined with shelves and cupboards. Leading to the back stairs, the passage gave access to both the attic and the cellar.

It was a long climb to the attic. The cellar was much nearer, down only one flight of steps. Although the door to the cellar stair was fitted with a lock, Sophie was pleased to discover that it was open. Cousin Robert often went down there for a last bottle of port before retiring. He preferred to make his own selection rather than leave the choice to Garrett, and he was careless about locking up behind himself.

On a shelf beside the door was a small oil lamp with the wick set low. Mrs Mayne always kept some light burning in the service areas, in case the servants were needed during the night. Sophie turned up the wick until a warm yellow light filled the glass chimney. Then, holding the lamp aloft, she started down.

The stairs were steep, with only a narrow handrail on one side. The bare brick walls smelled of damp. In Mama's day, Mrs Mayne would have been ordered to scrub those walls twice a year with carbolic solution. Now that Cousin Robert ran the house, standards were different. He only cared about what showed.

At the bottom of the steps was a row of unpainted timber doors. Each bore a small, neatly lettered sign: Buttery, Trunk Room, Tool Room, Coal. And one that read simply, Misc. Storage.

There was no lock on the storeroom door but the wood had warped, swelling in the frame. Opening it was difficult. Sophie set the lamp on the floor and tugged on the door handle with both hands. Nothing happened. She pulled harder. After a moment the door opened with a screech.

She picked up the lamp and stepped inside.

Shapes materialised from the darkness. Disused bits of furniture and garden equipment lay beside rolls of worn carpet. A battered brass birdcage, door ajar, mourned its missing canary. Propped in one corner was a wheelbarrow with its wheel missing. An old tin hip-bath held an assortment of worn cleaning brushes. Faded draperies which Mrs Mayne intended to make into something else someday were neatly stacked on wooden shelves, and …

… and …

Sophie gave a cry of delight. Protruding from one of the shelves was the handle of Nurse's dear old iron toasting fork! It was an omen, the first memory she would reclaim as her own.

Darting forward, she closed her fingers around the handle …

Chapter Seven

… just as another hand grasped it too.

The boy gave a cry of surprise and jumped back, but he did not turn loose of the metal bar. Never turn loose of anything valuable, that was his motto. Cobwebs plastered his face, veiling his eyes, clinging to his lips. Frantically he scraped them off …

And met the eyes of a red-haired girl not much older than himself. She was holding onto the other end of the metal bar, which he now recognised as a large, long-tined fork.

She was as startled as he was. 'Who are you?' she demanded to know.

'Who are you?' he replied, fear making his voice harsh. 'And what are you doing down here?'

'What am *I* doing here? *You* are the one with some explaining to do.'

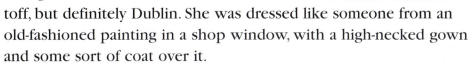

The girl's accent was a strange mixture of snob and toff, but definitely Dublin. She was dressed like someone from an old-fashioned painting in a shop window, with a high-necked gown and some sort of coat over it.

Then, suddenly, shockingly, Mickser realised that he could make out the outline of the brick wall behind her. He was seeing the bricks through her body. She was almost, but not quite, transparent.

'You're a ghost!' Mickser dropped the fork to bless himself.

At the same moment the girl shrieked and also turned loose of the fork.

And disappeared.

Mickser stared at the space where she had been. He had seen a ghost. Everyone knew the tenements were haunted. But he had seen one. A ghost.

Probably a banshee.

Probably come to warn him about his father's death.

Then the shakes began, and Mickser felt his legs give way.

When Sophie released the fork the boy was gone as abruptly as the candle blown out. Yet she knew she had seen him, she could recall every detail of his shabby clothes and starveling face, the look of shock in his black eyes.

She had been able to see *through* him …

Through him!

As her heart began to pound with terror, Sophie realised that she had seen a ghost.

She wanted to run from the cellar and never come back. She would run to Cook and tell her, 'I saw a ghost!' But then would Cook not send her to Mademoiselle?

Of course she would. And Mademoiselle would punish her for lying, or at the very least for having too much imagination. Mademoiselle did not believe young ladies should have imagination.

Sophie got as far as the foot of the stairs, then stopped and stood trembling, trying to think. 'Perhaps no one was there at all,' she told herself. 'Perhaps it was only a trick of the light, a fragment of a dream … '

But she knew that this had been no dream. She had seen him so clearly! A poor thin boy – or a ghost of a poor thin boy – all alone in the dark.

As she was alone.

She drew a long, shaky breath and went back to the storage room. Holding the lamp high, she cautiously surveyed the debris. No one hid there, no ghost lurked in the corner. Before her was merely a jumble of discarded objects, the unwanted and unloved.

Then Sophie's eyes fell on the toasting fork. Her newly found treasure.

She reached for the handle of the fork.

Mickser was used to being scared. There were a lot of things to fear in his life. He was afraid of the bigger boys in the street who beat him up; he was afraid of the way his belly felt when it cramped with hunger. He was afraid of stone bruises, those terrible boils that came up on bare feet. Most of all, he was afraid of his Daddy dying.

There were things that could hurt you, and things that couldn't. And ghosts couldn't. So there was no reason to be afraid of a ghost, he reasoned as he came shakily to his feet.

No reason.

His bare feet touched cool metal.

He was not going to give up a perfectly good piece of iron somebody might pay a ha'penny for, a ha'penny that could buy a bit of food for his Daddy.

Stooping, he grabbed the fork again.

He saw the hand first. Pale skin, translucent, perfect fingernails; a feminine right hand was wrapped around the other end of the fork. Mickser lifted his eyes …

She was there, staring at him, mouth open in amazement.

Instinct made him try to pull the fork from her grasp. 'I saw it first!' he said defiantly. 'So it's mine and you can't have it.'

She shook her head. 'It is mine. Nurse used to toast bread for me on this fork.'

'Nurse? You don't look sick to me.'

In spite of herself Sophie smiled. 'Not that sort of a nurse. I mean the woman who took care of me in the nursery.'

Mickser tightened his grip on the fork. 'Well this ain't your nursery. What I find down here is mine. Give it here!'

The girl's lips narrowed into a determined line. 'No.' With her left hand, she held up an oil lamp that shed a faint yellow light around him. She stared at him for a long moment by its glow, then put the lamp down again and took the fork handle in both hands and gave it a sharp tug.

'No!' Mickser reached out to push her away. His solid hand connected with her shoulder … and passed right through her flesh.

Sophie saw the gesture coming and flinched, bracing herself for the impact, but when he touched her she felt nothing.

Once again the children stared at one another.

'Are you dead?' Sophie asked in a whisper.

'No. I am not. Are you?'

'Certainly not! I am Sophie Marie Rutledge, aged fifteen years - almost sixteen - and I live at 19 Princess Sophie Mecklenburg Street. We share the same name, the street and I,' she added proudly. 'Except the street was named for King George's wife and I was named for my Grandmama.'

Mickser was fascinated by the way she spoke. Her accent was definitely Dublin, but very quaint and posh compared to his as he replied, 'This is 19 Railway Street, and I live here. Me, Mickser Lawless. With my family.'

'You live here?' The girl waved her arm around. 'You cannot possibly, we would have known. One of the servants would have seen you and reported it.'

The boy laughed scornfully. 'Servants? In this place?'

'There has been a full staff here ever since my Papa built this house,' she retorted.

'Your Papa built this house? When?'

'Shortly before he and Mama married in 1758, eighteen years ago. It was his wedding gift to her.'

Mickser felt his jaw drop. He did the sums quickly. 'That would make it 1776.' He saw the girl nod. 'But this is 1907!'

Children on the Oregon Trail

A. Rutgers van der Loeff

Chapter Two

John Sager is only thirteen when he and his family leave their Mississippi home to move to the Far West. John's father is convinced that a better life awaits them there. Travelling in a covered wagon train, they face many dangers on their journey.

That day began like any other.

At four o'clock in the morning, when the rising sun stood like a red-glowing ball above the grey landscape, the guards fired off their rifles, as a sign that the hours of sleep were past. Women, men and children streamed out of every tent and wagon; the gently smouldering fires from the previous night were replenished with wood, and bluish-grey clouds from dozens of plumes of smoke began to float through the morning air. Bacon was fried, coffee was made by those who still had some. The families which could still cook maize mush for the children thought themselves lucky.

All this took place within the 'corral', that was to say inside the ring which had been made by driving the wagons into a circle and fastening them firmly to each other by means of the shafts and chains. This formed a strong barricade through which even the most vicious ox could not break, and in the event of an attack by the Sioux Indians it would be a bulwark that was not to be despised.

Outside the corral the cattle and horses cropped the sparse grass in a wide circle.

At five o'clock sixty men mounted their horses and rode out of the camp. They fanned out through the crowds of cattle until they reached the outskirts of the herd; once there, they encircled the herd and began to drive all the cattle before them. The trained animals knew what those cracking whips meant, and what was required of them, and moved slowly in the direction of the camp. There the drivers picked their teams of oxen out from the dense mass and led them into the corral, where the yoke was put upon them.

From six o'clock until seven, the camp was extra busy; breakfast was eaten, tents were struck, wagons were loaded, and the teams of draught oxen and mules were made ready to be harnessed to their respective wagons and carts. Everyone knew that whoever was not ready when the signal to start was blown at seven o'clock would be doomed for that day to travel in the dusty rear of the caravan.

There were sixty-eight vehicles. They were divided into seventeen columns, each consisting of four wagons and carts. Each column took it in turn to lead the way. The section that was at the head today would bring up the rear tomorrow, unless a driver had missed his place in the row through laziness or negligence, and had to travel behind by way of punishment.

It was ten minutes to seven.

There were gaps everywhere in the corral; the teams of oxen were being harnessed in front of the wagons, the chains clanked. The women and children had taken their places under the canvas covers. The guide was standing among his assistants at the head of the line, ready to mount his horse and show the way. A dozen young men who were not on duty that day formed another group. They were going out buffalo-hunting; they had good horses and were well armed, which was certainly necessary, for the hostile Sioux had driven the herds of buffalo away from the River Platte, so that the hunters would be forced to ride fifteen or twenty miles to reach them.

As soon as the herdsmen were ready, they hurried to the rear of their herd, in order to drive them together and get them ready for today's march.

Seven o'clock.

An end had come to the busy running and walking to and fro, the cracking of whips, the shouts of command to the oxen, and the bawling from wagon to wagon – in short, to everything which, only just now, had appeared to be complete and utter chaos. Every driver was at his post. A bugle rang out! The guide and his escort mounted their horses; the four wagons of the leading section rumbled out of the camp and formed the first column, the rest took their places with the regularity of clockwork, and the caravan moved slowly forward over the broad plateau, far above the foaming river.

A new, hard day had begun. Particularly hard for the Sagers, who were having to do without the help of Mrs Ford, since she had gone to look after Walton's sick child.

The sun rose high in the sky. It was hot and stuffy under the canvas tilts, which were thick with dust. Towards noon the children everywhere began to bicker and whimper. But in the Sager family's wagon, they had other things to worry about.

John, who had been riding for hours in the blazing sun beside the heads of the foremost yoke of oxen, was given an order by his father, who was sitting on the driver's bench in the front of the wagon.

Immediately he galloped forward.

He had to fetch the doctor.

The doctor was a veterinary surgeon: the emigrants did not have a real doctor with them. But the vet had already done people a great deal of good, and helped them considerably, as well as animals.

John rode with all his might. Why on earth didn't the doctor travel in the middle of the caravan? From his father's face the boy had seen that the matter was urgent.

Meanwhile, Henry Sager had driven his wagon out of the line. He stopped.

'All the children must get out,' he ordered. 'Go and collect buffalo droppings and make a fire. Louise has to boil as much water as she can.'

Before Louise left the wagon, she filled the big kettle with water, scooping it up in a little tin bowl from the barrel in the back of the wagon. She cast a timid glance at her mother, who lay still and white on the tarpaulin. Mother caught Louise's eye and gave her a gentle, encouraging nod. If only that doctor would come quickly!

The doctor came.

With his long legs, he stepped from the saddle into the wagon in one stride. John tied up his horse. Then he wiped the sweat and dust out of his eyes with the back of his hand.

To the children, it seemed to take a long time. The water had already been boiling for quite a while. No one had asked for it yet, and they did not dare look into the wagon.

In the distance ahead of them hung a thick cloud of dust, behind which the caravan was hidden. They would fall very far to the rear. John looked worried. He knew that that was dangerous - stragglers ran the risk of being attacked; but he said nothing. Now and again his father came out and glanced around, scanned the trail behind them - eight sets of wagon wheels beside each other and thousands upon thousands of hoof marks. But behind, the horizon was clear and empty.

Until John suddenly perceived a tiny cloud of dust.

He started. He knew that that could only mean that Indians were approaching.

'Father!' he shouted.

Henry Sager stuck his head out of the wagon.

John pointed to the east, where the cloud of dust above their own tracks had now grown rather larger.

Father Sager said nothing.

He went back into the wagon with the kettle of boiling water, but came out again a moment later with five rifles and two pistols. John had already pulled his own pistol from its holster. His father gave him a rifle.

'All the children except John and Louise, get under the wagon,' he commanded quietly. But it was easy to see that that calmness of

his required all the self-control he had. His strong, wrinkled neck was fiery red, and the veins on his forehead were thick and purple.

'Take these,' he said to his eldest daughter, and Louise stood with three rifles in her arms, staring at the approaching cloud of dust as if turned to stone.

Father put the powder horn, lead, and ramrods down beside her.

John had laid his rifle across the saddlebow in front of him, as he had always seen the trappers do.

But his father said: 'Are you mad, boy? Get down and tie Mary up in front, along with the oxen. Do you want to serve as a target, and be shot out of the saddle?'

Francis pushed the smaller children under the wagon. Catherine began to resist, crying and kicking. 'Stop howling, you little idiot,' Francis snapped nervously, trying to make his voice sound as manly as possible. Matilda and Lizzy thought it rather a nice game; as a rule, they were never allowed to go under the wagon.

Father Sager climbed back in again.

He brought out two empty water casks, and the only bag of flour they had left. He stood the two casks upright beside the wagon, near one of the rear wheels, and laid the sack of flour across them.

'Come to the back here,' he ordered John and Louise. 'And remember – don't stir from cover. We fire along to one side of this, and between the casks … Louise, you load the rifles when we've fired them,' he said to her. To John he said nothing; he only looked at him.

A sound came from the wagon. It was like the crying of a tiny baby.

Father Sager gritted his teeth, and behaved as if he had not heard anything. The sound came again, more distinctly this time. Then he looked at his two eldest children; he almost had tears in his eyes.

'May God help us to protect that young life,' he said between clenched teeth. Rather more calmly, he went on: 'If it comes to that, it's not certain that the Indians mean mischief. And our rifles are good, sound ones. John, don't fire too soon, let 'em get close.'

He put his head back into the wagon.

'Don't worry, Doctor – we'll call if we can't manage without you.'

They waited in suspense. It was now easy to see that the cause of the cloud was horsemen – not many, perhaps half a dozen Indians on prairie ponies. They were superior in numbers, but they could not take cover anywhere.

There was no brushwood in which they could ensconce themselves.

'May God help us to protect that young life,' Father had said.

Windlord

MICHAEL SCOTT

Chapter Three: Chase

Long ago, Balor the wizard was Emperor of the Tuatha De Danann. So that none would oppose him, Balor sent out his dreaded Fomor warriors to capture all the other wizards and witches in his empire. In this extract the Windlord, Cian, and his family clash with Cichal, the leader of the Fomor warriors.

Cian raised his arms and called the wind with a word.

For a single moment nothing happened, and then abruptly, it was as if all the air had been sucked from the room, leaving a complete and terrifying silence. It lasted for the space of a single heartbeat, but when the air returned, it came in a deafening bang that shook the entire building. A howling wind swept across the floor of the library. It ripped the books from the shelves and sent them hurtling against the Fomor.

'I am the Windlord,' Cian said simply and the wind took and magnified his voice, sending it booming around the room. The storm grew in intensity as he spoke and was now visible as a greyish mist in the centre of the floor. 'I am the Lord of the Air; Master of the Wind.'

Whole sections of shelving were ripped free, their contents streaming through the air. Books, some of them covered in cloth and leather, or wood and hide, some bound in metal or thin slivers of stone, others wrapped in human skin, spun around the room in the tightly whirling tornado.

Cichal howled as the blizzard struck him, his great sword instinctively lashing out, slicing an enormous atlas in two. A series of large law books, each one bound in wood, struck him across the chest and head, sending him staggering backwards. He smashed into a bookcase in the middle of the floor, sending it toppling to the ground. The beast lost his footing and crashed down on top of it.

The air was filled with books now, spinning, twisting, turning, coiling, forcing the Fomor backwards towards the opening of the tunnel. The numerous volumes began to pile up around the entrance, blocking the hole. One of the serpent-folk broke through the barrier and ran screaming towards the steps leading up to the Windlords, but a metal-bound prayer-book struck him across the shins, doubling him over, and then a reading table crashed into him, actually picking him up off the ground, sending him tumbling across the polished floor.

Cichal crouched on all fours, using his barbed tail to help him keep his balance, digging his talons into the stone floor. The wind was a physical thing, stronger than the strongest warrior, pushing him backwards, his razor-sharp claws leaving deep furrows in the stone. The books were like slingshots, sharp, stinging and deadly. His six warriors were a match for a hundred of the human-kind, but they had no way of fighting the invisible elemental magic.

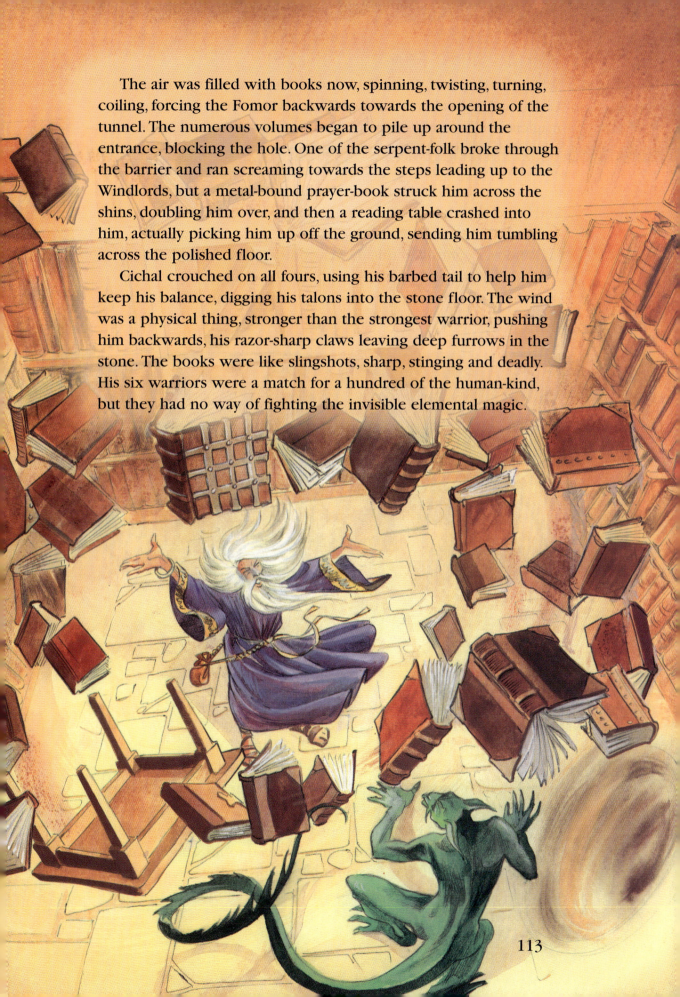

When the Emperor had told him to bring back this wind magician, Cichal had been almost insulted. There were other magicians, magicians who could raise the dead, command fire and stone, control demons – these were magicians with power, not some Windlord, whose only magic was to make the wind blow.

But crouched on the floor of Baddalaur's ancient library, bruised and bleeding, while the four human-kind fled higher into the building, Cichal understood the power of this wind magic.

Whoever controlled this power, controlled the world.

The Fomor smashed his fist into the floor, shattering a stone slab: there was nothing he could do … except wait. No magician could keep a spell working indefinitely.

'Help me,' Faolan gasped, staggering up the stairs, hauling the limp body of his father. The young boy's eyes were bright with tears. 'One moment he was fine, and then he just collapsed.'

Grannia came around her father's left side and draped his arm over her shoulder, while Etain raised her husband's head and lifted an eyelid. Only the white was showing.

'Lay you father here.' She swept a book-laden table free with her arm and together the three of them managed to lift Cian up onto the table. Etain lifted his wrist and felt for his pulse. It was faint and ragged. 'What happened, Faolan?' she asked. 'Tell me exactly what happened.'

'He had called up the wind and used it to drive the Fomor back,' Faolan began.

'How did he call up the wind?' Etain interrupted.

The boy looked up at her in surprise. 'He just raised his hands and began.'

Etain drew a sharp breath, tears magnifying her eyes.

'Mother ... mother? What's wrong?' Faolan demanded, but it was Grannia who answered. She had already begun her training in the Windlore, and knew some of the dangers involved in raising the wind.

'You cannot call the wind just like that,' she said quietly. 'It needs time and preparation. The Windlore is one of the four elemental magics, like fire, earth and water. It draws its power from within the magician, unlike other forms of magic which use special ingredients. If the magician isn't prepared physically and mentally to work the spell, then the elemental magic will destroy him. It will just use him up.' Her eyes darted to the unconscious form of her father. His chest was barely moving and there was blood on his lips. She looked at her mother. 'What are we going to do?'

Etain shook her head. 'I don't know,' she said tiredly.

There was a sudden crash from below and Faolan ran to the railing, looking down into the devastated hallway below. The Fomor had broken out of the tunnel again and were now advancing through the rubble towards the steps.

'They're coming,' he gasped. 'We've got to go ... '

'Your father cannot be moved,' Etain said firmly.

'But the Fomor ... ' Grannia began.

'The Fomor want us alive; they won't harm us. They know if anything happens us, the Emperor will have their heads.'

'But what are we going to do?' Faolan whispered. They could hear the beasts' claws rasping on the wooden stairs.

'You two will have to flee ... ' Both Grannia and Faolan started to shake their heads, but Etain pressed on. 'Go north into the Ice-Fields of Thusal. In a village close to the Top of the World you'll find your uncle, Lugh. He is the last of the Windriders. Give him this.' She pressed a small ancient-looking book into Faolan's hands. 'This is the Book of the Wind. It is so ancient that legend has it that the gods themselves wrote it. It contains the Windlore; whoever reads this book will know the secret of the wind. They could become a Windlord. It must not fall into the Emperor's hands.

Find your uncle, tell him what has happened; tell him we need his help now.' She leaned over and kissed them both, 'Now go. Go!'

Both Grannia and Faolan shook their heads.

'You have to go,' Etain insisted. 'The wind is the most powerful of the elemental magics; if the Emperor controls it, he can control the world.'

'I'm staying,' Grannia said simply. She looked at Faolan. 'You go. One person will have a better chance of evading the beasts than two, and besides, you know no magic. They won't be able to track you that way.'

Puzzled, Faolan looked at his mother.

'Every little use of magic disturbs the natural world, like a pebble dropped into a pool,' Etain explained. 'A good magician will be able to track another user of magic across many hundreds of leagues. Grannia is right. She has used magic, she would be easy to track.' Etain reached out her hand and held it close to her daughter's face. 'I can feel the power flowing off her from here.' She leaned forward and kissed her son on the forehead. 'You'll have to go alone, Faolan. You are our only hope.'

The beasts were so close now that they could smell their sour, snake smell.

'Go now, Faolan. Protect the book with your life. Whatever you do, don't let it fall into the Emperor's hands … destroy it if you have to, but only as a last resort. Now go! We'll try to hold them here.'

Blinking furiously, Faolan came to his feet. The Fomor were on the stairs, moving cautiously now that they had learned of the Windlord's power.

He kissed his mother quickly and hugged his sister, and then leaned across his father and kissed his cold clammy cheek. 'I'll be back,' he whispered into his ear. 'I'll come back for you.'

The White Mountains

JOHN CHRISTOPHER

Chapter Two: My Name is Ozymandias

At fourteen, Will will be Capped and become a man. There will be great feasting and a Tripod will visit the village. Massive, alien machines, the Tripods have ruled the Earth for thousands of years. Can Will escape this fate?

I went to the den after school with mingled feelings of anticipation and unease. My father had said he hoped he would hear no more reports of my mixing with Vagrants, and had placed a direct prohibition on my going to the Vagrant House. I had obeyed the second part, and was taking steps to avoid the first, but I was under no illusion that he would regard this as anything but wilful disobedience. And to what end? The opportunity of talking to a man whose conversation was a hodge-podge of sense and nonsense, with the latter very much predominating. It was not worth it.

And yet, remembering the keen blue eyes under the mass of red hair, I could not help feeling that there was something about this man that made the risk, and the disobedience, worth while. I kept a sharp look-out on my way to the ruins, and called out as I approached the den. But there was no one there; nor for a good time after that. I began to think he was not coming - that his wits were so addled that he had failed to take my meaning, or forgotten it altogether - when I heard a twig snap and, peering out, saw Ozymandias. He was less than ten yards from the entrance. He was not singing, or talking, but moving quietly, almost stealthily.

A new fear struck me then. There were tales that a Vagrant once, years ago, had murdered children in a dozen villages, before he was caught and hanged. Could they be true, and could this be such another? I had invited him here, telling no one, and a cry for help would not be heard as far from the village as this. I froze against the wall of the den, tensing myself for a rush that might carry me past him to the comparative safety of the open.

But a single glance at him as he looked in reassured me. Whether mad or not, I was sure this was a man to be trusted. The lines in his face were the lines of good humour. He said: 'So I have found you, Will.' He glanced about him, in approval. 'You have a snug place here.'

'My cousin Jack did most of it. He is better with his hands than I am.'

'The one that was Capped this summer?'

'Yes.'

'You watched the Capping?' I nodded. 'How is he, since then?'

'Well,' I said, 'but different.'

'Having become a man.'

'Not only that.'

'Tell me.'

I hesitated a moment, but in voice and gesture as well as face he inspired confidence. He was also, I realised, talking naturally and sensibly, with none of the strange words and archaic phrases he had used previously. I began to talk, disjointedly at first and then with more ease, of what Jack had said, and of my own later perplexity. He listened, nodding at times but not interrupting. When I had finished, he said: 'Tell me, Will - what do you think of the Tripods?'

I said truthfully: 'I don't know. I used to take them for granted - and I was frightened of them, I suppose - but now ... There are questions in my mind.'

'Have you put them to your elders?'

'What good would it do? No one talks about the Tripods. One learns that as a child.'

'Shall I answer them for you?' he asked. 'Such as I can answer.'

There was one thing I was sure of, and I blurted it out: 'You are not a Vagrant!'

He smiled. 'It depends what meaning you give that word. I go from place to place, as you see. And I behave strangely.'

'But to deceive people, not because you cannot help it. Your mind has not been changed.'

'No. Not as the minds of the Vagrants are. Nor as your cousin Jack's was, either.'

'But you have been Capped!'

He touched the mesh of metal, under his thatch of red hair. 'Agreed. But not by the Tripods. By men - free men.'

Bewildered, I said: 'I don't understand.'

'How could you? But listen, and I will tell you. The Tripods, first. Do you know what they are?' I shook my head, and he went on: 'Nor do we, as a certainty. There are two stories about them. One is that they were machines, made by men, which revolted against men and enslaved them.'

'In the old days? The days of the giant ship, of the great-cities?'

'Yes. It is a story I find hard to believe, because I do not see how men could give intelligence to machines. The other story is that they do not come originally from this world, but another.'

'Another world?'

I was lost again. He said: 'They teach you nothing about the stars in school, do they? That is something that perhaps makes the second story more likely to be the true one. You are not told that the stars at night - all the hundreds of thousands of them - are suns like our own sun, and that some may have planets circling them, as our earth circles this sun.'

I was confused, my head spinning with the idea. I said: 'Is this true?'

'Quite true. And it may be that the Tripods came, in the first place, from one of those worlds. It may be that the Tripods themselves are only vehicles, for creatures who travel inside them. We have never seen the inside of a Tripod, so we do not know.'

'And the Caps?'

'Are the means by which they keep men docile and obedient to them.'

At first thought, it was incredible. Later, it seemed incredible that I had not thought this before. But all my life Capping had been something I had taken for granted. All my elders were Capped, and contented to be so. It was the mark of the adult, the ceremony itself solemn and linked in one's mind with the holiday and the feast. Despite the few who suffered pain and became Vagrants, it was a duty to which every child looked forward. Only lately, as one could begin to count the months remaining, had there been any doubts in my mind; and the doubts had been ill-formed and difficult to sustain against the weight of adult assurance. Jack had had doubts, too, and then, with the Capping, they had gone. I said: 'They make men think the things the Tripods want them to think?'

'They control the brain. How, or to what extent, we are not sure. As you know, the metal is joined to the flesh, so that it cannot be removed. It seems that certain general orders are given when the Cap is put on. Later, specific orders can be given to specific people, but as far as the majority are concerned, they do not seem to bother.'

'How do the Vagrants happen?'

'That again is something at which we can only guess. It may be that some minds are weak to start with, and crumble under the strain. Or perhaps the reverse: too strong, so that they fight against domination until they break.'

I thought of that, and shuddered. A voice inside one's head, inescapable and irresistible. Anger burned in me, not only for the Vagrants but for all the others - my parents and elders, Jack ...

'You spoke of free men,' I said. 'Then the Tripods do not rule all the earth?'

'Near enough all. There are no lands without them, if that's what you mean. Listen, when the Tripods first came - or when they revolted - there were terrible happenings. Cities were destroyed like ant-hills, and millions on millions were killed or starved to death.'

Millions ... I tried to envisage it, but could not. Our village, which was reckoned no small place, numbered about four hundred souls. There were some thirty thousand living in and around the city of Winchester. I shook my head.

He went on: 'Those that were left the Tripods Capped, and once Capped they served the Tripods and helped to kill or capture other men. So, within a generation, things were much as they are now. But in one place, at least, a few men escaped. Far to the south, across the sea, there are high mountains, so high that snow lies on them all the year round. The Tripods keep to low ground - perhaps because they travel over it more easily, or because they do not like the thin air higher up - and these are places which men who are alert and free can defend against the Capped who live in the surrounding valleys. In fact, we raid their farms for our food.'

'We? So you come from there?' He nodded. 'And the Cap you wear?'

'Taken from a dead man. I shaved my head, and it was moulded to fit my skull. Once my hair had grown again, it was hard to tell it from a true Cap. But it gives no commands.'

'So you can travel as a Vagrant,' I said, 'and no one suspects you. But why? With what purpose?'

'Partly to see things, and report what I see. But there is something more important. I came for you.'

I was startled. 'For me?'

'You, and others like you. Those who are not yet Capped, but who are old enough to ask questions and understand answers. And to make a long, difficult, perhaps dangerous journey.'

'To the south?'

'To the south. To the White Mountains. With a hard life at the journey's end. But a free one. Well?'

'You will take me there?'

'No. I am not ready to go back yet. And it would be more dangerous. A boy travelling on his own could be an ordinary runaway, but one travelling with a Vagrant … you must go on your own. If you decide to go.'

'The sea,' I said, 'how do I cross that?'

He stared at me, and smiled. 'The easiest part. And I can give you some help for the rest, too.' He brought something from his pocket and showed it to me. 'Do you know what this is?'

I nodded. 'I have seen one. A compass. The needle points always to the north.'

'And this.'

He put his hand inside his tunic. There was a hole in the stitching, and he put his fingers down, grasped something, and drew it out. It was a long cylinder of parchment, which he unrolled and spread out on the floor, putting a stone on one end and holding the other. I saw a drawing on it, but it made no sense.

'This is called a map,' he said. 'The Capped do not need them, so you have not seen one before. It tells you how to reach the White Mountains. Look, there. That signifies the sea. And here, at the bottom, the mountains.'

He explained all the things on the map, describing the landmarks I should look for and telling me how to use the compass to find my way. And for the last part of the journey, beyond the Great Lake, he gave me instructions which I had to memorise. This in case the map were discovered. He said: 'But guard it well, in any case. Can you make a hole in the lining of your tunic, as I have done?'

'Yes. I'll keep it safe.'

'That leaves only the sea crossing. Go to this town.' He pointed to it. 'You will find fishing boats in the harbour. The *Orion* is owned by one of us. A tall man, very swarthy, with a long nose and thin lips. His name is Curtis, Captain Curtis. Go to him.

He will get you across the sea. That is where the hard part begins. They speak a different language there. You must keep from being seen, or spoken to, and learn to steal your food as you go.'

'I can do that. Do you speak their language?'

'It, and others. Such as your own. It was for that reason I was given this mission.' He smiled. 'I can be a mad man in four tongues.'

I said: 'I came to you. If I had not … '

'I would have found you. I have some skill in discovering the right kind of boy. But you can help me now. Is there any other in these parts that you think might be worth the tackling?'

I shook my head. 'No, no one.'

He stood up, stretching his legs and rubbing his knee. 'Then tomorrow I will move on. Give me a week before you leave, so that no one suspects a link between us.'

'Before you go … '

'Yes?'

'Why did they not destroy men altogether, instead of Capping them?'

He shrugged. 'We can't read their minds. There are many possible reasons. Part of the food you grow here goes to men who work underground, mining metals for the Tripods. And in some places, there are hunts.'

'Hunts?'

'The Tripods hunt men, as men hunt foxes.' I shivered. 'And they take men and women into their cities, for reasons at which we can only guess.'

'They have cities, then?'

'Not on this side of the sea. I have not seen one, but I know those who have. Towers and spires of metal, it is said, behind a great encircling wall. Gleaming ugly places.'

I said: 'Do you know how long it has been?'

'That the Tripods have ruled? More than a hundred years. But to the Capped, it is the same as ten thousand.' He gave me his hand. 'Do your best, Will.'

'Yes,' I said. His grasp was firm.

'I will hope to meet you again, in the White Mountains.'

Poetry

Contents • Poetry

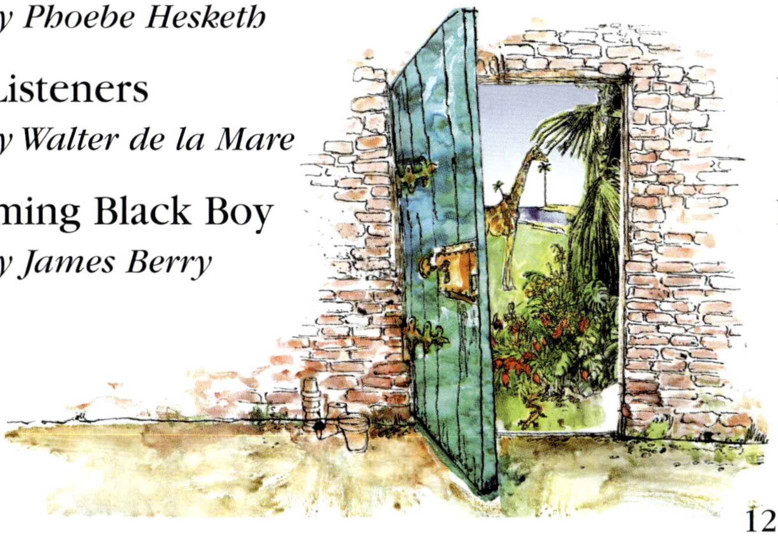

Through That Door

Through that door
Is a garden with a wall,
The red brick crumbling,
The lupins growing tall,
Where the lawn is like a carpet
Spread for you,
And it's all as tranquil
As you never knew.

Through that door
Is the great ocean-sea
Which heaves and rolls
To eternity,
With its islands and promontories
Waiting for you
To explore and discover
In that vastness of blue.

Through that door
Is your secret room
Where the window lets in
The light of the moon,
With its mysteries and magic
Where you can find
Thrills and excitements
Of every kind.

Through that door
Are the mountains and the moors
And the rivers and the forests
Of the great outdoors,
All the plains and the ice-caps
And lakes as blue as sky
For all those creatures
That walk or swim or fly.

Through that door
Is the city of the mind
Where you can imagine
What you'll find.
You can make of that city
What you want it to,
And if you choose to share it,
Then it could come true.

JOHN COTTON

The New Kid on the Block

There's a new kid on the block,
and boy, that kid is tough,
that new kid punches hard,
that new kid plays real tough,
that new kid's big and strong,
with muscles everywhere,
that new kid tweaked my arm,
that new kid pulled my hair.

That new kid likes to fight,
and picks on all the guys
that new kid scares me some,
(that new kid's twice my size),
that new kid stomped my toes,
that new kid swiped my ball,
that new kid's really bad,
I don't care for her at all.

JACK PRELUTSKY

Playgrounds

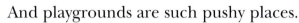

Playgrounds are such gobby places.
Know what I mean?
Everyone seems to have something to
Talk about, giggle, whisper, scream and shout about.
I mean, it's like being in a parrot cage.

And playgrounds are such pushy places.
Know what I mean?
Everyone seems to have to
Run about, jump, kick, do cartwheels, handstands, fly around.
I mean, it's like being inside a whirlwind.

And playgrounds are such patchy places.
Know what I mean?
Everyone seems to
Go round in circles, lines and triangles, coloured shapes.
I mean, it's like being in a kaleidoscope.

And playgrounds are such pally places.
Know what I mean?
Everyone seems to
Have best friends, secrets, link arms, be in gangs.
Everyone, except me.

Know what I mean?

BERLIE DOHERTY

This Orange Tree

I touched my first rose
Under this orange tree,
I was young and fruity
The sweet rose was blooming.

I found faith
Under this orange tree
It was here all the time.
One day I picked it up
Then I realized
How great you are.

It was under this
Very orange tree
That I read
My first Martin Luther King speech.
How great the word.

It was here
Under this very orange tree,
On this very peace of earth
That I first sang
With a hummingbird.
How great the song.

This orange tree knows me,
It is my friend,
I trust it and
It taste good.

BENJAMIN ZEPHANIAH

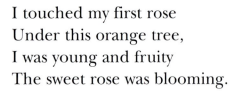

Secrets

I have a secret, but I hide
This information deep inside,
Where no one else can see – but me.
– I keep it hidden,
Carefully.

For deep inside me, many things
Soar jewel-bright on tender wings;
Protected in a magic land
That only I can understand.
And thoughts and feelings ebb and flow
Untrammelled where they seek to go;
Where rainbows ribbon through the sky,
And I can catch them if I try.
All this is mine, and mine alone,
A kingdom of my very own.

– And so I hide my secrets here,
Where no one else can interfere;
Where only I can ever see,
I keep them hidden,
– Carefully!

MARGOT BOSONNET

And It's A …

Miller gets the ball and
d
r
i
b
b
l
e
s

d
o
w
n

the

w
i
n
g

b a s   f   a   a k e   from Smith
e t   o f   t c l

On no! He's lost it!
r
i
a
the
in
up
it
s
e
o
WAIT! He t

s it to – oh – kcab ti sessap eh.
d
a
e
h

A lovely c
u
r
v
i
n
g kick

AND IT'S A …

wONDerful S-A-A-A-A-A-A-A-A-A-V-E!

RITA RAY

Translation

Miller gets the ball and dribbles down the wing,
beats off a tackle from Smith.
Oh no! He's lost it!
Wait! He toes it up in the air,
heads it to – oh – he passes it
back. A lovely curving kick.
And it's a wonderful save!

The Wayfarer

The beauty of the world hath made me sad,
This beauty that will pass;
Sometimes my heart hath shaken with great joy
To see a leaping squirrel in a tree,
Or a red lady-bird upon a stalk,
Or little rabbits in a field at evening,
Lit by a slanting sun,
Or some green hill where shadows drifted by,
Some quiet hill where mountainy man hath sown
And soon will reap, near to the gate of Heaven;
Or children with bare feet upon the sands
Of some ebbed sea, or playing on the streets
Of little towns in Connacht,
Things young and happy.
And then my heart hath told me:
These will pass,
Will pass and change, will die and be no more,
Things bright and green, things young and happy;
And I have gone upon my way
Sorrowful.

Padraic Pearse

Sky in the Pie!

Waiter, there's a sky in my pie
Remove it at once if you please
You can keep your incredible sunsets
I ordered mincemeat and cheese

I can't stand nightingales singing
Or clouds all burnished with gold
The whispering breeze is disturbing the peas
And making my chips go all cold

I don't care if the chef is an artist
Whose canvases hang in the Tate
I want two veg. and puff pastry
Not the Universe heaped on my plate

OK I'll try just a spoonful
I suppose I've got nothing to lose
Mm ... the colours quite tickle the palette
With a blend of delicate hues

The sun has a custardy flavour
And the clouds are as light as air
And the wind a chewier texture
(With a hint of cinnamon there?)

This sky is simply delicious
Why haven't I tried it before?
I can chew my way through to Eternity
And still have room left for more

Having acquired a taste for the Cosmos
I'll polish this sunset off soon
I can't wait to tuck into the night sky
Waiter! Please bring me the Moon!

ROGER MCGOUGH

On Ageing

When you see me sitting quietly,
Like a sack left on the shelf,
Don't think I need your chattering,
I'm listening to myself.
Hold! Stop! Don't pity me!
Hold! Stop your sympathy!
Understanding if you got it,
Otherwise I'll do without it!

When my bones are stiff and aching
And my feet won't climb the stairs,
I will only ask one favour:
Don't bring me no rocking chair.

When you see me walking, stumbling,
Don't study and get it wrong.
'Cause tired don't mean lazy
And every goodbye ain't gone.
I'm the same person I was back then,
A little less hair, a little less chin,
A lot less lungs and much less wind,
But ain't I lucky I can still breathe in.

MAYA ANGELOU

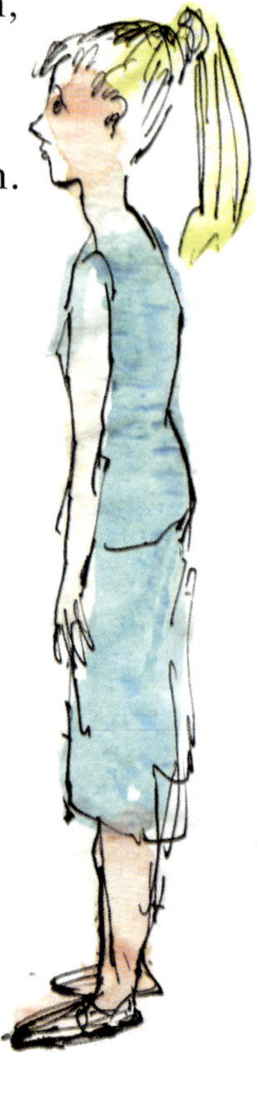

Twelve Songs IX

Stop all the clocks, cut off the telephone,
Prevent the dog from barking with a juicy bone,
Silence the pianos and with muffled drum
Bring out the coffin, let the mourners come.

Let aeroplanes circle moaning overhead
Scribbling on the sky the message He Is Dead,
Put crepe bows round the white necks of the public doves,
Let the traffic policemen wear black cotton gloves.

He was my North, my South, my East and West,
My working week and my Sunday rest,
My noon, my midnight, my talk, my song;
I thought that love would last for ever: I was wrong

The stars are not wanted now: put out every one;
Pack up the moon and dismantle the sun;
Pour away the ocean and sweep up the wood.
For nothing now can ever come to any good.

W.H. Auden

When All the Others

When all the others were away at Mass
I was all hers as we peeled potatoes.
They broke the silence, let fall one by one
Like solder weeping off the soldering iron:
Cold comforts set between us, things to share
Gleaming in a bucket of clean water.
And again let fall. Little pleasant splashes
From each other's work would bring us to our senses.

So while the parish priest at her bedside
Went hammer and tongs at the prayers for the dying
And some were responding and some crying
I remembered her head bent towards my head,
Her breath in mine, our fluent dipping knives –
Never closer the whole rest of our lives.

SEAMUS HEANEY

The Flower-Fed Buffaloes

The flower-fed buffaloes of the spring
In the days of long ago,
Ranged where the locomotives sing
And the prairie flowers lie low;
The tossing, blooming, perfumed grass
Is swept away by wheat,
Wheels and wheels and wheels spin by
In the spring that still is sweet.
But the flower-fed buffaloes of the spring
Left us long ago.
They gore no more, they bellow no more,
They trundle around the hills no more:
With the Blackfeet, lying low,
With the Pawnees, lying low.

VACHEL LINDSAY

The Bogeyman

In the desolate depths of a perilous place
the bogeyman lurks, with a snarl on his face.
Never dare, never dare to approach his dark lair
for he's waiting ... just waiting ... to get you.

He skulks in the shadows, relentless and wild
in his search for a tender, delectable child.
With his steely sharp claws and his slavering jaws
oh he's waiting ... just waiting ... to get you.

Many have entered his dreary domain
but not even one has been heard from again.
They no doubt make a feast for the butchering beast
and he's waiting ... just waiting ... to get you.

In that sulphorous, sunless and sinister place
he'll crumple your bones in his bogey embrace.
Never never go near if you hold your life dear,
for oh! ... what he'll do ... when he gets you!

JACK PRELUTSKY

Whatif

Last night, while I lay thinking here,
Some Whatifs crawled inside my ear
And pranced and partied all night long
And sang their same old Whatif song:
Whatif I'm dumb in school?
Whatif they've closed the swimming-pool?
Whatif I get beat up?
Whatif there's poison in my cup?
Whatif I start to cry?
Whatif I get sick and die?
Whatif I flunk that test?
Whatif green hair grows on my chest?
Whatif nobody likes me?
Whatif a bolt of lightning strikes me?
Whatif I don't grow taller?
Whatif my head starts getting smaller?
Whatif the fish won't bite?
Whatif the wind tears up my kite?
Whatif they start a war?
Whatif my parents get divorced?
Whatif the bus is late?
Whatif my teeth don't grow in straight?
Whatif I tear my pants?
Whatif I never learn to dance?
Everything seems swell, and then
The night-time Whatifs strike again!

SHEL SILVERSTEIN

Getting Up Early

Getting up early promises well:
A milkhorse on the road
Induces thoughts of a sleeping world
And a waking God.

This hour has something sacred;
Bells will be ringing soon,
But now I am content to watch
The day begin to bloom.

I would only waste my breath
On poor superfluous words;
How perfectly they sing for me –
The new invisible birds

Who celebrate the light that spreads
Like love to window sills,
As morning steps like a laughing girl
Down from the Dublin hills.

Brendan Kennelly

He Wishes for the Cloths of Heaven

Had I the heavens' embroidered cloths,
Enwrought with golden and silver light,
The blue and the dim and the dark cloths
Of night and light and the half-light,
I would spread the cloths under your feet:
But I, being poor, have only my dreams;
I have spread my dreams under your feet;
Tread softly because you tread on my dreams.

W.B. YEATS

A Piece of Sky

There was this child,
Not very old,
Who looked at the sky
Blue pink and gold,
And wanted a piece,
Just a pie-sized slice,
To hold.
He knew just how it would feel.
Treasure heavy it would weigh
And magic, it would change colour
With the day
From light to dark, from blue to grey.
He didn't want to keep it,
Just to borrow,
They could put it back again,
He said,
Tomorrow.
They questioned him with what and why.
The sky,
He said
Was like a dome that fitted the earth
Exactly half-way down.
It drew the horizon,
Outlined the trees,
Held down the mountains
And stemmed the seas.
And the tide?
Too many people on one side
Of the world,
East or West, South or North,
Tilted it and made the seas slop back and forth.

And cloud?
Cloud was fog on holiday.
And fog?
Fog was cloud, the other way.
And rainbows?
Rainbows were the ghosts of lights
That people switched off
In the middles of nights.
And …?
He tired of questions
He was ready for bed
He didn't know everywhere he said.
Their questions really made him sigh
All he wanted was a piece of sky.
They explained the world to him.
Told him the what and where and why
Of cloud and rainbows, sky and tide
Until he thought his brains were fried.
Then he smiled at them, politely sceptic
After all, their explanation of the world
Was too fantastic.

JULIE HOLDER

Creatures

The butterfly, alive inside a box,
Beats with its powdered wings in soundless knocks
And wishes polythene were hollyhocks.

The beetle clambering across the road
Appears to find his body quite a load:
My fingers meddle with his highway code

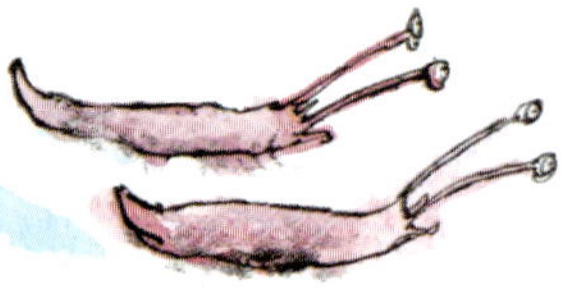

And slugs are rescued from the fatal hiss
Of tyres that kiss like zigzagged liquorice
On zigzagged liquorice, but sometimes miss.

Two snails are raced across a glistening stone
(Each eye thrust forward like a microphone)
So slowly that the winner is unknown.

To all these little creatures I collect
I mean no cruelty or disrespect
Although their day-by-day routine is wrecked.

They may remember their experience,
Though at the time it made no sort of sense,
And treat it with a kind of reverence.

It may be something that they never mention,
An episode outside their apprehension
Like some predestined intervention.

JOHN FULLER

The Lake Isle of Innisfree

I will arise and go now, and go to Innisfree,
And a small cabin build there, of clay and wattles made:
Nine bean-rows will I have there, a hive for the honey-bee,
And live alone in the bee-loud glade.

And I shall have some peace there, for peace comes dropping slow,
Dropping from the veils of the morning to where the cricket sings;
There midnight's all a glimmer, and noon a purple glow,
And evening full of the linnet's wings.

I will arise and go now, for always night and day
I hear lake water lapping with low sounds by the shore;
While I stand on the roadway, or on the pavements grey,
I hear it in the deep heart's core.

W.B. YEATS

Shed in Space

My Grandad Lewis
On my mother's side
Had two ambitions.
One was to take first prize
For shallots at the village show
And the second
Was to be a space commander.

Every Tuesday
After I'd got their messages,
He'd lead me with a wink
To his garden shed
And there, amongst the linseed
And the sacks of peat and horse manure
He'd light his pipe
And settle in his deck chair.
His old eyes on the blue and distant
That no one else could see,
He'd ask,
'Are we A OK for lift off?'
Gripping the handles of the lawn mower
I'd reply:
'A OK'

And then
Facing the workbench,
In front of shelves of paint and creosote
And racks of glistening chisels
He'd talk to Mission Control.
'Five-Four-Three-Two-One-Zero –
We have lift off.
This is Grandad Lewis talking,
Do you read me?
Britain's first space shed

Is rising majestically into orbit
From its launch pad
In the allotments
In Lakey Lane.'

And so we'd fly,
Through timeless afternoons
Till tea time came,
Amongst the planets
And mysterious suns,
While the world
Receded like a dream:
Grandad never won
That prize for shallots,
But as the captain
Of an intergalactic shed
There was no one to touch him.

GARETH OWEN

Truant

Sing a song of sunlight
My pocket's full of sky –
Starling's egg for April
Jay's feather for July.
And here's a thorn bush three bags full
Of drift-white wool.

They call him dunce, and yet he can discern
Each mouse-brown bird,
And call its name and whistle back its call,
And spy among the fern
Delicate movement of a furred
Fugitive creature hiding from the day.
Discovered secrets magnify his play
Into a vocation.

Laughing at education
He knows when the redshank hides her nest, perceives
a reed-patch tremble when a coot lays seige
To water territory.
Nothing escapes his eye:
A ladybird
Slides like a blood-drop down a spear of grass;
The sapphire sparkle of a dragon-fly
Redeems a waste of weeds.
Collecting acorns, telling the beads of the year
On yew tree berries, his mind's too full for speech.

Back in the classroom he can never find
Answers to dusty questions, yet could teach,

Deeper than knowledge,
Geometry of twigs
Scratched on a sunlit wall;
History in stones,
Seasons told by the fields' calendar –
Living languages of Spring and Fall.

PHOEBE HESKETH

The Listeners

'Is there anybody there?' said the Traveller,
    Knocking on the moonlit door;
And his horse in the silence champed the grasses
    Of the forest's ferny floor:
And a bird flew up out of the turret,
    Above the Traveller's head:
And he smote upon the door again a second time;
    'Is there anybody there?' he said.
But no one descended to the Traveller;
    No head from the leaf-fringed sill
Leaned over and looked into his grey eyes,
    Where he stood perplexed and still.
But only a host of phantom listeners
    That dwelt in the lone house then
Stood listening in the quiet of the moonlight
    To that voice from the world of men:

Stood thronging the faint moonbeams on the dark stair
    That goes down to the empty hall,
Hearkening in an air stirred and shaken
    By the lonely Traveller's call.
And he felt in his heart their strangeness,
    Their stillness answering his cry,
While his horse moved, cropping the dark turf,
    'Neath the starred and leafy sky;
For he suddenly smote on the door, even
    Louder, and lifted his head: –
'Tell them I came, and no one answered,
    That I kept my word,' he said.
Never the least stir made the listeners,
    Though every word he spake
Fell echoing through the shadowiness of the still house
    From the one man left awake:
Ay, they heard his foot upon the stirrup,
    And the sound of iron on stone,
And how the silence surged softly backward,
    When the plunging hoofs were gone.

WALTER DE LA MARE

Dreaming Black Boy

I wish my teacher's eyes wouldn't
go past me today. Wish he'd know
it's okay to hug me when I kick
a goal. Wish I myself wouldn't
hold back when an answer comes.
I'm no woodchopper now
like all ancestors.

I wish I could be educated
to the best of tune up, and earn
good money and not sink to lick
boots. I wish I could go on every
crisscross way of the globe
and no persons or powers or
hotel keepers would make it a waste.

I wish life wouldn't spend me out
opposing. Wish same way creation
would have me stand it would have
me stretch, and hold high, my voice
Paul Robeson's, my inside eye
a sun. Nobody wants to say
hello to nasty answers.

I wish torch throwers of night
would burn lights for decent times.
Wish plotters in pyjamas would pray
for themselves. Wish people wouldn't
talk as if I dropped from Mars.

I wish only boys were scared
behind bravados, for I could suffer
I could suffer a big big lot.
I wish nobody would want to earn
the terrible burden I can suffer.

James Berry

Drama

Contents • Drama

School For Thieves

MICHAEL AND MOLLIE HARDWICK

This play is an adaptation of Oliver Twist *a novel by Charles Dickens. Oliver is an orphan who has to make his own way in the world. In this extract, Oliver has been forced to join up with a gang of thieves led by the scheming Fagin.*

CAST

Charles Dickens
Oliver Twist
Jack Dawkins (The Artful Dodger)
Fagin
Charley Bates
Three more of Fagin's boys

Dawkins Got any lodgings?

Oliver No.

Dawkins Money?

Oliver No. Do you live in London?

Dawkins I do when I'm at home. I suppose you want someplace to sleep tonight, don't you?

Oliver I do indeed. I haven't slept under a roof since I left the country.

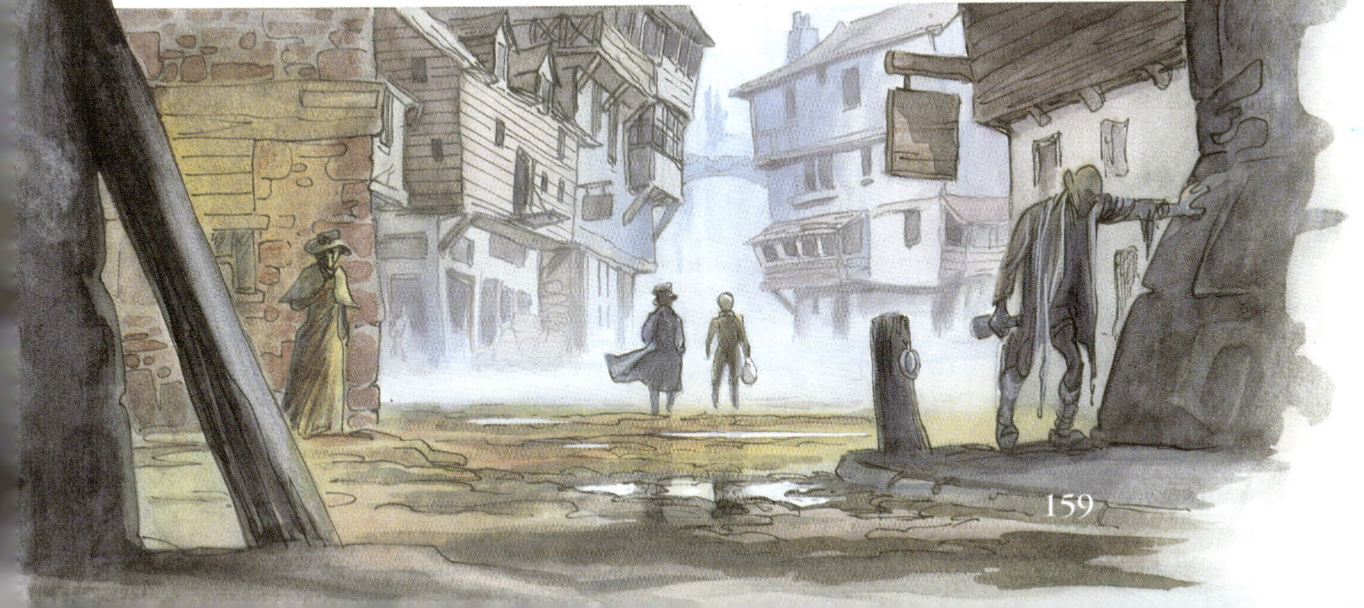

Dawkins Well, don't fret your eyelids on that score. I've got to be in London tonight, and I know a 'spectable old gen'lman as lives there wot'll give you lodgings for nothink, and never ask for the change. That is, if any gen'lman he knows introduces you.

Oliver Does he know you?

Dawkins Don't he? Oh, no! Not in the least! By no means! Certainly not! Come on, young shaver, and you'll see if Jack Dawkins and 'is friend is welcome or not. I'm at low water-mark myself - only a bob in my pocket - but you want some grub first, and you shall have it.

Dickens Assisting Oliver to rise, the young gentlemen took him to an adjacent shop, where he purchased ham and a loaf. Oliver made a hearty meal, after which they set forth together on the road to London.
The Artful Dodger, as Jack Dawkins explained he was known to his intimate friends, led the way at a rapid pace through Islington into Saffron Hill. A dirtier or more wretched place Oliver had never seen. The street was very narrow and muddy, children screamed everywhere and drunken men and women positively wallowed in filth. Oliver was just considering whether he hadn't better run away when the Dodger caught him by the arm, pushed open the door of a house and drew him quickly inside. The walls and ceiling of the room were black with age and dirt. In front of the fire was a very old, shrivelled man, with a villainous-looking face and dressed in a greasy flannel gown. Four boys, smoking long clay pipes and drinking spirits with the air of middle-aged men, were sorting a great number of silk handkerchiefs at a table.

Dawkins Hullo, Fagin.

Fagin Dodger, my dear! but there's two of you.

Dawkins This here's my friend, Oliver Twist.

Fagin (*bowing low*) Oliver, eh? We're very glad to see you, Oliver, very. One of you take Oliver's cap and hang it up for him. Somebody give him a chair near the fire. And keep them hands out of his pockets, or I'll lay this toasting-fork across you! Ah, Oliver, my dear, you're a-starin' at the handkerchiefs, I see. There are a good many of 'em, ain't there? We've just looked 'em out ready for the wash, eh, lads?

All except Oliver laugh heartily.

Charley Bates here made all these – didn't you, Charley?

Laughter again.

He's a good boy, ain't you, Charley? Very well *made*. Only you ain't marked some of 'em too well. The marks will have to be picked out again with a needle.

More laughter.

Perhaps we'll teach Oliver how to do it, eh? Shall us, Oliver?

Oliver If you please, sir.

Fagin You'd like to be able to make pocket handkerchiefs as easy as Charley, wouldn't you, my dear?

Oliver Very much indeed, if you'll teach me, sir.

Loud laughter from the rest.

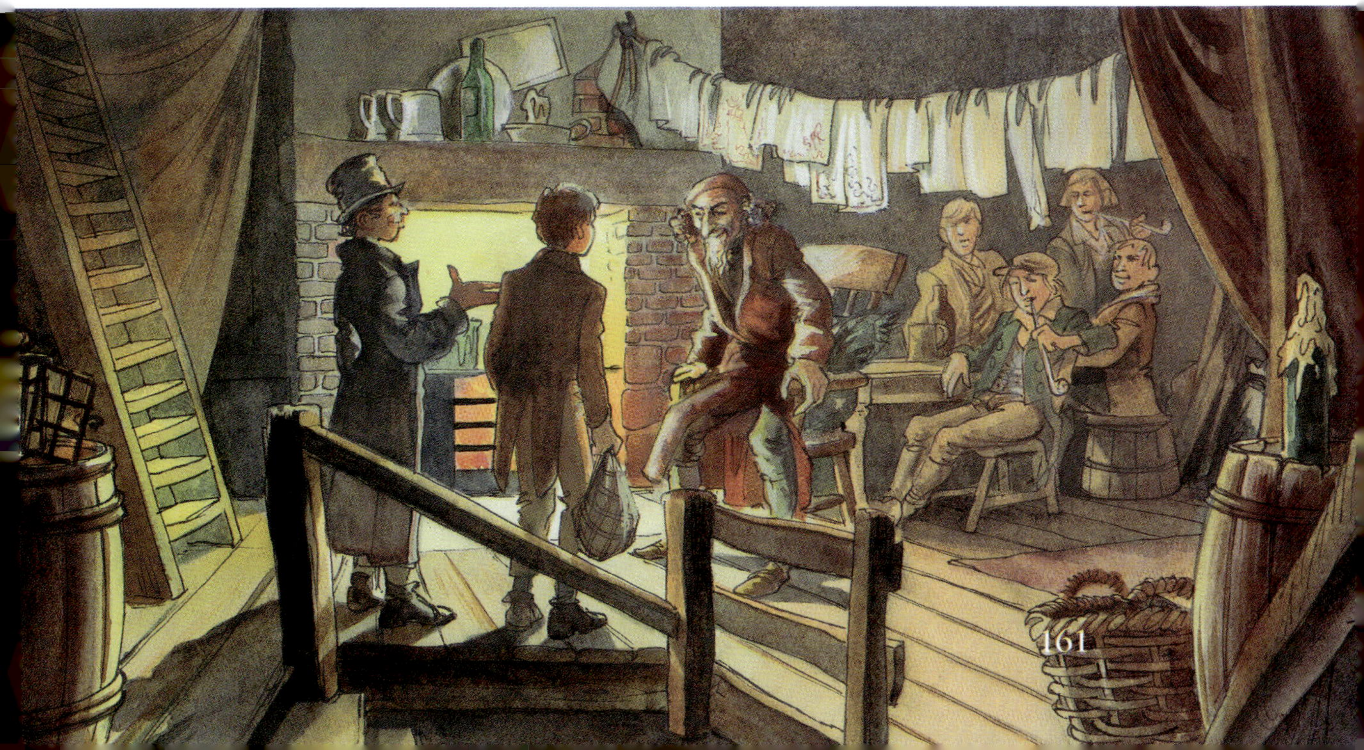

Fagin Now, Dodger, I hope you've been working hard today?

Dawkins Hard as nails, Fagin.

Fagin Good boy, good boy. What have you made?

Dawkins A couple of wallets.

Fagin Well *lined*, I hope?

Dawkins Pretty well. Here they are.

Fagin Hm! Not quite so heavy as they might be. But very neat and nicely made. Ingenious workman, ain't he, Oliver?

Oliver Very indeed, sir.

Laughter.

Fagin Well, all work and no play … It's time for our game, boys. Dodger and Charley first.

Others Yes!

Fagin You sit and watch, Oliver, and then you can learn to play.

Dickens Placing a snuff-box in one pocket of his trousers, a wallet in another, and a watch in his waistpocket, and sticking a diamond pin in his shirt, Fagin buttoned his coat tight round him. Having put his spectacle-case and handkerchief in his coat pockets, he took a stick and trotted up and down the room in imitation of the manner in which old gentlemen walk about the streets. Sometimes he stopped at the fireplace, and sometimes at the door, making believe that he was

staring with all his might into shop windows. At such times he would look constantly round him, for fear of thieves, and would keep slapping all his pockets in turn, to see that he hadn't lost anything, in such a very funny and natural manner that Oliver laughed till the tears ran down his face. All this time the Dodger and Charley followed him closely about, getting out of his sight nimbly every time he turned round.

At last the Dodger trod upon his toes, as though accidentally, while Charley Bates stumbled up against him behind; and in that one moment they took from him, with the most extraordinary rapidity, snuff-box, wallet, watch, diamond pin, and spectacle-case. But as Charley was removing the handkerchief, Fagin cried out and seized his wrist, and then the things had to be put back and the game begun all over again with two of the other boys.

Fagin (*to Oliver*) There, my dear, that's a pleasant game, isn't it?

Oliver Oh, very good, sir.

Laughter.

Fagin Is my handkerchief hanging out of my pocket, my dear?

Oliver Yes, sir.

Fagin Then see if you can take it out without my feeling it, as you saw them do.

Oliver gingerly takes the handkerchief, Fagin winking at the other boys unseen by him.

Is it gone yet?

Oliver Yes, sir. Here it is.

Fagin My word, what a clever boy! I never saw a sharper boy. Here's a shilling for you, my dear.

Oliver Thank you, sir!

Fagin If you go in this way you'll be the greatest man of the time. And now, the rest of you, be off!

The Scottish Play

BY STAN BARRETT

CAST	**Narrator**	**Beth**
	Tim	**Fergus**
	Witch 1/ Emma	**Witch 2/ Jo**
	Witch 3/ Sam	

Narrator We are in a village hall a few days before the Christmas pantomime 'Jack and the Beanstalk'. Outside it is dark, wet and windy. Fergus, an old man, is painting the scenery. He stops when he hears three slow, loud knocks. Beth and Tim burst through the door.

Beth It's all right, Fergus, it's only us. Wow! It's terrible out there. Hey, Fergus! That scenery! It's brilliant!

Narrator The old man, who never speaks, nods and smiles.

Tim (*not really interested*) I suppose that's Jack's garden.

Beth The bushes look dead real!

Tim That's because they are real.

Beth They're terrific.

Tim Brilliant. Where's the beanstalk?

Narrator Fergus points to a huge plant pot, then he disappears backstage.

Beth You see? The beanstalk's going to grow out of that pot.

Narrator As Beth stares at the stage, Tim starts to search through his sister's school bag.

Beth (*looking annoyed*) Hey! What are you doing in my bag?

Tim Looking for the script.

Beth You don't need a script. If you'd learnt your lines properly, we wouldn't need this extra rehearsal!

Tim Ah! Here's one.

Beth That's not it! That's 'Mac …' (*she pauses nervously*) I mean that's 'The Scottish Play'. We're doing it at school.

Tim It says here it's called 'Macbeth' and it's by William Shakespeare.

Beth (*holding her finger to her lips*) Shhh! When you're in a theatre you never say its title. Our teacher told us.

Tim Why not? Anyway, this isn't a theatre.

Beth It is now. It's got a stage, scenery and lights, so it's a theatre. You don't say its title and you don't quote words from it. It's bad luck. Strange things can happen.

Tim I don't believe it.

Beth Well, you should.

Tim You're just superstitious. Anyway, how could you rehearse it without quoting words from it?

Beth That's different. It doesn't count when you're actually rehearsing the play.

Narrator Beth looks at the book over Tim's shoulder. She tells him that the story is about murder and black magic. Macbeth is a warrior who wants to be king.
He plans to murder the old Scottish king, then blame it on the servants.

Tim It sounds better than 'Jack and the Beanstalk'.
But look at it! I can't understand a word.

Beth (*in her grown-up's voice*) You will when you're older. That is how Shakespeare wrote in his time.

Tim What? You mean the actors all talked like this?
(*starts to read slowly in a very flat voice*) 'Thrice the brinded cat hath mew'd. Thrice and once the hedge-pig whin'd'.

Narrator They hear three slow, heavy knocks from the stage. They spin round to see Fergus. He is banging the stage floor with a brush handle. The old man glares at Tim and puts a finger to his lips. Then, he draws his finger across his throat.

Beth It's all right, Fergus. It's just Tim. He didn't know. He won't do it again.

Narrator Fergus stares hard at Tim. Then, shaking his head, disappears into the darkness backstage.

Tim What was all that about?

Beth Fergus heard you quoting from 'Mac ...' 'The Scottish Play', and he got upset.

Tim (*quietly*) What a load of rubbish!

Narrator Suddenly, there is a crash of thunder and the lights go out.

Tim Beth! I can't see!

Beth Tim! Look at the stage!

Narrator There is a red glow underneath the huge plant pot. By its light, three black-hooded figures gather round the pot. The thunder rumbles on.

The witches sound like old women, but their voices are loud and clear

Witch 1 Thrice the brinded cat hath mew'd.

Witch 2 Thrice and once the hedge-pig whin'd.

Witch 3 Harpier cries: 'Tis time, 'tis time.

Narrator There is another crash of thunder. Beth and Tim clap their hands over their ears. The red glow bursts into blue and yellow flames that lick the bottom of the pot. The three figures hum softly as they circle slowly round the fire.

Tim (*in a loud whisper*) Beth, who are they? What's happening?

Beth I can't believe this. They are the three witches from the play.

Tim What play?

Beth The Scottish Play'!

Tim	What are they doing?
Beth	Casting a spell to read Mac …, his future. Get down and be quiet. I don't think they know we're here.
Witch 1	Round about the cauldron go; In the poison'd entrails throw. Toad that under cold stone Days and night has thirty-one Swelter'd venom, sleeping got Boil thou first i' th' charmed pot.
Witch 1 **Witch 2** **Witch 3**	Double, double, toil and trouble; Fire burn and cauldron bubble.
Narrator	The witches circle the pot still humming. Beth and Tim are sitting on the floor. They curl up and try to look as small as they can.
Tim	(*moans*) Beth, I don't like this.
Beth	It's all your fault! I told you strange things might happen!

Witch 2 Fillet of a fenny snake,
In the cauldron boil and bake;
Eye of newt, and toe of frog,
Wool of bat, and tongue of dog,
Adder's fork, and blind-worm's sting,
Lizard's leg and howlet's wing,
For a charm of pow'rful trouble,
Like a hell-broth boil and bubble.

Witch 1
Witch 2
Witch 3 Double, double, toil and trouble;
Fire burn and cauldron bubble.

Narrator As the witches circle and hum, Tim gets over his fear and starts to creep nearer to the centre of the stage.

Beth (*in a soft but urgent whisper*) Tim! Come back!

Tim (*in a loud whisper*) I don't think this is real. It's just somebody acting.

Narrator The pot bubbles and spits as if it is angry. There is a deafening crash of thunder from outside that shakes the village hall. Tim scrambles back to join Beth in a huddle on the floor.

Witch 3 Scale of dragon, tooth of wolf,
Witches' mummy, maw and gulf
Of the ravin'd salt-sea shark,
Root of hemlock digg'd i' th' dark …

Narrator Tim crawls towards the door with Beth trying to pull him back.

Beth (*in an urgent whisper*) Tim! Keep still. They'll see us!

Tim They've seen us already.

Beth (*alarmed*) They're coming.

Tim I'm going!

Narrator As they chant, two of the witches slip to the door and bar Tim's way out.

Witch 1
Witch 2
Witch 3 Double, double, toil and trouble;
Fire burn and cauldron bubble.

Witch 2 Cool it with a baboon's blood,
Then the charm is firm and good.

Narrator Tim shakes himself free of Beth. He turns to look for the fire exit. The third witch takes a branch from the stage and bars his way.

Beth Look out!

Narrator The other two witches are moving in behind him. The third witch steps closer, waves the branch at him and throws her hood back. Beth screams as she sees a horrible mask of a baby's face with a crown on its head.

Tim	Beth! What's ... what's happening?
Witch 1 **Witch 2**	Listen, but speak not to 't.
Narrator	The third witch points out at Tim. She speaks to him as if he were Macbeth.
Witch 3	Macbeth shall not vanquish'd be until Great Birnam Wood to high Dunsinane Hill Shall come against him.
Witch 1 **Witch 2**	That will never be.
Tim	Look! I don't know what you're on about and I don't care. I'm going home. Right?
Narrator	But before Tim can move, the two witches behind him suddenly whip off their cloaks and throw them over him. Tim struggles and falls in a heap on the floor.
Tim	(*his voice muffled*) Help! Let me out!
Narrator	Tim stops shouting when he hears laughter. Even his sister is laughing.
Beth	(*relieved*) Emma! Jo! And Sam! It was you all the time! And I never knew! Those voices didn't sound at all like yours.
Sam	(*proudly*) That's good acting for you.
Narrator	Tim finally gets his head free. The lights are back on and he stares at the three 'witches'. They are Beth's school friends.

Emma Had you fooled there, didn't we?

Jo You all right, Tim? Sorry about that, but we know Beth is superstitious. We knew she'd fallen for all that bad luck stuff in 'Macbeth'.

Tim You mean it's not true?

Sam Of course it's not true. Not unless you're superstitious. Like Beth.

Beth No, I'm not. Not really. Anyway, how come Fergus didn't stop you? He believes in it.

Emma I know he does but we asked him if we could rehearse the witches' scene round that big pot.

Jo We told him it was for drama at school.

Emma So he didn't mind. He even found us those old black-curtains.

Sam And that wicked baby mask and crown.

Emma And he put the lights out. That's when we got the idea of trying to fool you.

Tim I don't know why, but I got really scared when you were waving that branch at me. What was that all about?

Sam Now, that was funny. I hadn't learnt that bit. I hadn't even looked at it, but the words just came out. It was as if something inside was telling me what to say.

Jo Yeah. And how did we know to say: 'That will never be', at the end? That must be Macbeth's line.

Emma (*shrugs*) Don't know. It just came out. Strange, isn't it?

Beth Stop it, you three. It's creepy.

Tim But what did it mean?

Beth Well, Mac …, he wants the witches to tell him if he is safe from his enemies now he is king.

Tim So he did murder the old Scottish king?

Emma Yes, but Lady Macbeth planted the murder weapon on the servants.

Tim Lady Macbeth? Who's she?

Beth His wife. She wanted to be queen so she urged her husband to kill the old man.

Jo Mind you, she went completely mad afterwards. In her sleep she kept trying to wash the old king's blood off her hands when there was none there.

Sam And she went around saying things like: (*in an actor's voice*) 'Out, damned spot!' and 'Here's the smell of the blood still'.

Beth Sam! Don't!

Emma Oh, come on, Beth. You don't really believe all that stuff.

Beth Fergus does. If he hears you, he'll throw us out.

Tim (*impatiently*) But you still haven't told me about the branch.

Emma The witches told Macbeth that he would be safe until Birnam Wood moved to the hill at Dunsinane.

Jo Macbeth thought this would never happen.

Beth But the rebel army chopped down the trees and hid behind the branches as they marched towards Dunsinane.

Sam So the forest of trees moved!

Tim Wow! What happens next?

Beth (*interrupting*) Look! Look at the stage! The bushes are moving!

Narrator They stand and stare in disbelief until they see Fergus. He is only moving the scenery round.

Jo Wow! That's a relief! For a minute, I thought …

Emma Hey! I've just remembered something my mum once told me about Fergus. (*continues quietly so that Fergus can't hear*) He used to be a stage manager in the West End.

Tim West end of what?

Beth Oh come on, Tim. The West End of London. That's where all the big theatres are. Go on, Emma.

Emma Well, one day he said to three actresses who were playing the witches in 'Macbeth': 'How now, you secret, black and midnight hags!'

Beth I wish you wouldn't do that, Emma.

Emma I have to. It's part of the story. And ever since then, he's never spoken a single word.

Jo Mind you, nobody believes it.

Sam There's more than that. They say that Fergus can speak, but only lines from 'Macbeth'. It's all a load of rubbish if you ask me.

Emma I expect you're right. Well, come on you two. We'll let Beth and Tim get on with their pantomime rehearsal.

Tim Hang on a minute! How did you manage all that thunder?

Beth Yes. And that fire under the pot? It looked so real.

Sam Thunder? What thunder?

Jo There wasn't any thunder.

Beth (*getting cross*) Of course there was! It made the whole building shake, didn't it, Tim?

Sam There was no fire either. Just a little red light that Fergus gave us to put under the pot.

Beth (*angrily*) Oh come on, you three! We know what we saw, don't we Tim?

Emma Beth! Just calm down a minute. I think you're winding us up to get your own back.

Tim Beth's telling the truth. We heard real thunder and saw real flames.

Emma That's weird. Really weird. I think we should go. All of us. Right now, before anything else happens.

Tim But we haven't rehearsed our scene in 'Jack' yet.

Beth We'll do it at home. (*loudly*) Cheers, Fergus. And thanks for letting us in.

Narrator Fergus waves to the children as they go. He stands on the stage and stares into space. He is startled by three slow, loud bangs and three dark, shadowy shapes as they gather round the pot. He speaks: 'How now, you secret, black and midnight hags!'

Acknowledgements

Prose

The Phantom Tollbooth by Norton Juster, used by permission of HarperCollins Publishers; *Flight of the Doves* by Walter Macken, used by permission of Macmillan Publishers; *The Animal, The Vegetable and John D. Jones* by Betsy Byars, published by The Bodley Head 1982, used by permission of The Random House Group; *Tom's Midnight Garden* by Philippa Pearce, used by permission of Oxford University Press; *Timesnatch* by Robert Swindells, used by permission of Transworld Publishers; *No Gun for Asmir* by Christobel Mattingly, used by permission of Penguin Books Australia; *The Ghost of Thomas Kempe* © Penelope Lively 1973, first published by Heinemann Young Books, an imprint of Egmont Children's Books and used with permission; *The Great Gilly Hopkins* by Katherine Paterson (Victor Gollancz/Hamish Hamilton, 1979) Katherine Paterson 1978; *Me and Nu: A Childhood at Coole* by Anne Gregory, used by permission of Colin Smythe Ltd; *Thunder and Lightnings* by Jan Mark (Kestrel, 1976), © Jan Mark 1976, used by permission of Penguin Books; *The Ghost of Grania O'Malley* © 1996 Michael Morpurgo, first published by Mammoth, an imprint of Egmont Children's Books and used with permission; *The Hobbit* by J R R Tolkien, used by permission of HarperCollins Publishers; *The Deerstone* by Maeve Friel, used by permission of Poolbeg Press; *The Exiles* by Hilary McKay, used by permission of Hodder and Stoughton Ltd; *19 Railway Street* by Michael Scott and Morgan Llywelyn, used by permission of Poolbeg Press; *Children on the Oregon Trail* by A Rutgers van der Loeff, used by permission of Hodder and Stoughton Ltd; *Windlord* by Michael Scott, used by permission of Wolfhound Press; *The White Mountains* by John Christopher, used by permission Sam Youd.

Poetry

New Kid on the Block © Jack Prelutsky 1984, published in the UK by Heinemann Young Books, an imprint of Egmont Children's Books and used with permission; *Playgrounds* by Berlie Doherty, used by permission of David Higham Associates; *This Orange Tree* from *Funky Chickens* by Benjamin Zephaniah (Viking, 1996), © Benjamin Zephaniah 1996; *Secrets* by Margot Bosonnet, from *Skyscraper Ted*, used by permission of Wolfhound Press; *And It's A ...* by Rita Ray, used by permission of Macmillan Publishers; *Sky in the Pie!* by Roger McGough reprinted by permission of PFD on behalf of Roger McGough, © Roger McGough as printed in the original volume; *Twelve Songs IX* by W H Auden from *Collected Poems* by W H Auden, used by permission of Faber and Faber Ltd; *When All the Others* (extract from *Clearances 111*) from *The Haw Lantern* by Seamus Heaney, used by permission of Faber and Faber Ltd; *The Bogeyman* by Jack Prelutsky, from *Nightmares, Poems to Trouble your Sleep* by Jack Prelutsky; *Whatif* from *A Light in the Attic* by Shel Silverstein, used by permission of Edite Kroll Literary Agency; *Getting Up Early* by Brendan Kennelly, used by permission of the author; *He Wishes for the Cloths of Heaven* by W B Yeats, used by permission of A P Watt Ltd on behalf of Michael B Yeats; *A Piece of Sky* by Julie Holder, from *A Third Book of Poetry* compiled by John Foster, published by Oxford University Press, used by permission of the author; *The Lake Isle of Inishfree* by W B Yeats, used by permission of A P Watt on behalf of Michael B Yeats; *The Listeners* by Walter de la Mare, used by permission of The Literary Trustees of Walter de la Mare and the Society of Authors as their representative.

Drama

School for Thieves by Michael and Mollie Hardwick, used by permission of John Murray; *The Scottish Play* by Stan Barrett, reprinted by permission of Heinemann Educational Publishers, a division of Reed Educational and Professional Publishing Ltd.

Every effort has been made to trace copyright holders but we would be glad to rectify any omissions at the next reprint.